WILDERNESS B

ALSO BY ANTHONY BURTON

A Programmed Guide to Office Warfare
The Jones Report
The Canal Builders
The Reluctant Musketeer
Canals in Colour
Remains of a Revolution
The Master Idol   The Navigators   A Place to Stand
Josiah Wedgwood
Canal (*with Derek Pratt*)
The Miners
Back Door Britain
Industrial Archaeological Sites of Britain
The Green Bag Travellers (*with Pip Burton*)
The Past at Work
The Rainhill Story
The Past Afloat
The Changing River
The Shell Book of Curious Britain
The National Trust Guide to Our Industrial Past
The Waterways of Britain
The Rise & Fall of King Cotton
Walking the Line

Anthony Burton

WILDERNESS BRITAIN

with photographs by Jorge Lewinski

ANDRE DEUTSCH

CONTENTS

First published 1985 by André Deutsch Limited
105 Great Russell Street London WC1

Text Copyright © 1985 by Anthony Burton
Photographs Copyright © 1985 by Jorge Lewinski
All rights reserved

ISBN 0 233 97640 X

Printed and bound in Great Britain

For all my walking companions,
but especially for Pip
who suffered blisters in a good cause

John O'Groats
Wick
Fashven
12
Helmsdale
Ullapoole
Tain
Elgin
Fraserburgh
Inverness
Invershiel
11
Cairn Gorm
Aberdeen
Fort William
Ben Nevis
Rannoch
Moor
Glencoe
St Andrews
Glasgow
Edinburgh
Ayr

1 Otmoor
2 Bodmin Moor
3 Dartmoor
4 The Ancient Lands
5 Mid Wales
6 North Wales
7 Breck, Fen and Marsh
8 The Peak District
9 The Pennines
10 The Lake District
11 The Highlands
12 Cape Wrath

● Towns and Villages
▲ Mountains
⊙ Archaeological Monument

Newcastle-upon-Tyne
9
Keswick Skiddaw
Langdale Ambleside
10 Windermere
Pen-y-Ghent
Malham York
Marsden
Huddersfield
7
Edale
Llandudno Liverpool Kinder Scout Lincoln
Buxton
8
Bethseda Chester Matlock
Llanberis Pass Snowdon Boston
Pwllehui Cromford
Llangollen Derby Kings Lynn
6 Norwich
Birmingham Thetford
Dylife West Stow
Aberystwyth Wicken 7
Pennont 5
Llandrindod
Cardigan Wells
Gloucester 1
Noke Oddington
Oxford
Cardiff Fyfield
Avebury Marlborough London
Bristol Silbury Hill
⊙ Stonehenge
4 Salisbury

Oakhampton Belstone
Camelford 3
Wadebridge South Brent
2 Torquay
Bodmin
St. Neot Plymouth
Penzance

Wilderness, wildness – descriptive terms known to us all, yet they are terms capable of a multitude of interpretations. To some, a wild place is simply a spot untouched by civilization, a place fit only for barbarians with no care for culture and decent values. To others it might represent one of the few remaining resorts of innocence, a fragment of the earth's surface untouched by the corruption that forms an inescapable part of all man's works. These are extreme views, admittedly, but if you look backwards over the years, you will find that they are far from modern views. Cast your eye over the literary horizon and you will see striding across it – though in opposite directions – two giants of the world of letters. There goes Samuel Johnson, stomping along on the way south, heading for the delights of the capital, for books, for theatres and for the conversation of his peers. His visit to the Highlands of Scotland afforded him much of interest in the way of subjects for philosophy, but little to delight the eye or gladden the heart.

> Of the hills many may be called with Homer's Ida *abundant in springs*, but few can deserve the epithet which he bestows upon Pelion by *waving their leaves*. They exhibit little variety; being almost wholly covered with dark heath, and even that seems to be checked in its growth. What is not heath is nakedness, a little diversified by now and then a stream rushing down the steep. An eye accustomed to flowery pastures and waving harvests is astonished and repelled by this wide extent of hopeless sterility. The appearance is that of matter incapable of form or usefulness, dismissed by nature from her care and disinherited of her favours, left in its original elemental state or quickened only with one sullen power of useless vegetation. [*A Journey to the Western Islands of Scotland*]

Passing him on the way north goes William Wordsworth, no less eager in his return to Grasmere and the hills. He was as prone to philosophic musings as was Johnson, but the musings took a different form and the hill scenery affected the poet in very different ways:

> 'Ah! what a sweet recess', thought I, 'is here!'
> Instantly throwing down my limbs at ease
> Upon a bed of heath – 'full many a spot
> Of hidden beauty I chanced t'espy
> Among the mountains; never one like this;
> So lonesome, and so perfectly secure:
> Not melancholy – no, for it is green,
> And bright, and fertile, furnish'd in itself

With the few needful things that life requires.
In rugged arms how soft it seems to lie,
How tenderly protected! Far and near
We have an image of the pristine earth,
The planet in its nakedness; were this
Man's only dwelling, sole appointed seat,
First, last, and single, in the breathing world,
It could not be more quiet: peace is here
Or nowhere.

[*The Excursion*]

Two views then that are as different as can be, or so it would seem at first glance. Yet is this so? Both are alike in accepting the subjective nature of their judgement on the wild places they visited; both were aware that it was man's relationship with the landscape that was being judged, and not the 'pure' landscape itself. It is easy, too easy, to deal in stereotyped images, and by selective quotation one has grossly

The limestone cliffs of Malham Cove.

oversimplified the views of two great writers. Continue reading Johnson, and this passage will be found:

> 'We were in this place by ease and by choice, and had no evils to suffer or to fear; yet the imaginations excited by the view of an unknown and untravelled wilderness are not such as arise in the artificial solitude of parks and gardens, a flattering notion of self-sufficiency, a placid indulgence of voluntary delusions, a secure expansion of the fancy, or a cool concentration of the mental powers.'

And when Wordsworth wrote 'Earth has not anything to show more fair', it was the early morning view of London that he was describing. There is no simple answer to the question of how we should define, let alone describe, wild places.

If it is difficult to define wilderness, it is not a great deal easier to analyse its appeal. There is, it is true, a series of popular assumptions about the countryside – that it is somehow more 'real' than the town, that older values such as community spirit are preserved there and still to be seen at work. Such views rarely pass close scrutiny. The village community has largely been broken: weekenders occupy the old labourers' cottages and commuters the farm houses, though there is an undeniable reality about the atmosphere at that time of the year when the liquid manure is being sprayed on the fields. It is also frequently said that the countryside offers a relief from the pressures of modern life and here, at any rate, we stand on surer ground, for in one particular area those pressures can not only be described but can be measured – and in the modern world where statistics form the new *lingua franca* this surely makes the case irrefutable.

Britain has become steadily more crowded over the years. The population density of England and Wales was, according to the 1801 census, 58.86 per square kilometre: we should not enquire too closely into those figures, but they are probably of the right order. By 1971 the density had risen to 321.68 or, in other words, where one human being had stood at the beginning of the last century, half a dozen were now elbowing into the same space. And that is only a part of the story, for the pattern within the country has changed as well with a steady drift of population into towns and cities. The overall density statistics look bad enough, but when you turn to Greater London and find not three hundred-odd in that square kilometre but four-and-a-half thousand, then it does seem that there is indeed a measurable pressure at work in modern life. And, of course, so many of those thousands are all trying to do the same thing at the same time – all sitting in the same traffic jams on the way into work, packing into the same buses and trains and repeating the whole dose over again on the homeward journey of the evening. How many of us, looking at, say, Oxford Street in the January sales, have viewed the jostling thousands and longed for a magic wand that would make the crowds vanish leaving just ourselves and a few friends to wander the streets in peace and comfort – producing, shall we say, a population density of seven per square kilometre. And that is just the figure we find for the Highland Region of Scotland.

Not surprisingly, those looking for an escape from the crowds turn to such areas as the Highlands. But do they find a wilderness? That depends very much on subjective impressions, that difficult problem of defining a wilderness. We do not have any vast tracts of untamed land – no Himalayan range, no Saharan desert, no Amazonian jungle – but no one who has ever stood alone in the centre of Dartmoor watching the approach of darkly swollen rain clouds could ever doubt the statement that it is possible to find wild, and even dangerous, country in Britain. We can also say that small though our wild places may be when viewed on a world scale they do boast a wonderfully rich diversity.

Some years ago I travelled across Canada by train from the east coast to the west. It was thrilling to steam through the great forest, but somewhat less thrilling to wake the next morning to see what appeared to be the same trees outside the carriage window. Then came the prairies, and a very great deal of wheat, to be followed, at last, by the mountains. The Rockies are spectacularly beautiful, but I found that this division of land into huge, clearly defined chunks diminished the appeal of the particular place. It was a landscape without surprises. Now the British landscape on the other hand is full of surprises, small-scale though they may be – and surely only the most crass equate size with beauty. A Mahler symphony is different from a Mozart sonata – not necessarily either better or worse – merely different. The glories of the British landscape lie in the variety and richness of small pleasures which add up to a unique whole.

You can see something of that diversity on any map, but if you turn to a geological map you can see the basis on which it is built. I own a splendid example of such a map, printed in colour so that the whole country is slashed through with varying tones as brash and gaudy as a Neapolitan ice cream. Here you can see all the rocks that poke through the surface: rough, hard gabbros and granites, crumbling chalk and softly moulded sandstone; and all those others which though they remain deeply hidden give shape to the land above. And these underground changes are reflected too in many of the works of man, especially those which were made in a time when building materials were found literally at one's own doorstep. This has an immense visual effect. For example, the gleaming limestone of the Yorkshire–Lancashire border gives a feeling of great lightness to the country in

contrast to the lowering gritstone further to the east. These regional differences are absolutely vital to the appeal of the British landscape and their erosion in recent times has had a devastating effect. Shortly before writing these words I was staying with friends in Yorkshire and was looking out from their house to the moorland dotted with stone farmhouses and striped with dark walls rising up the hillside. It was an inhabited land and yet it felt a wild land precisely because of this harmony of material, man using the land in a very direct manner. Then my eyes turned towards the valley head. A modern bungalow had been built out of brick and at once all sense of wildness vanished and the moors were reduced to the status of a suburban appendage – just one building, and a landscape had been transformed.

The problem of retaining the true country, the country where everything belongs together is one that must be solved if the unique British landscape is to be preserved. Happily there are a number of bodies who recognize this need. The National Trust is an excellent example. It is often thought of primarily in terms of fine buildings

Near the Wash and Long Sutton.

which the general public can go and visit, but when the Trust was formed in 1895 it was given this full title: The National Trust for Places of Historic Interest or Natural Beauty. They have been dealing with both aspects ever since, but one is less aware of their ownership of land to which the public have free access than one is of the houses where tickets are handed out at the door. As recently as 1983 they took over the care and stewardship of Kinder Scout to add to the considerable area of moorland, woodland, mountain and coast for which they already had responsibility. Through such schemes some at least of our wild areas appear to be safe. And the schemes are also an indication that the Trust still cares about both halves of their title and recognizes that the two are, in fact, not just equally important but indivisible. History lies as much in the land as in ancient monuments or country mansions.

We might seem to have strayed some way from our original definition of wildness and questions about its appeal, but we have in fact come some way towards an understanding. The importance and appeal of wilderness areas must lie in a combination of history and natural beauty. Britain is a country geographically tiny almost to the point of insignificance; but historically rich almost to surfeit. No part of the land is truly wild, nowhere untouched by man and his past. Those who go to the wilderness to find relief from the civilization we have built over the centuries, will inevitably find themselves stumbling across reminders of that same long process of development. And they will just as surely find that man is still imposing new patterns on the land. To set down 'civilization' and 'wilderness' as opposites is false; a wilderness may be found within earshot of a busy road, while Wordsworth's daffodils might well be growing within the ruins of a past age.

In this brief survey of some of the wild places of Britain, there is no attempt to reach encyclopædic completeness. If there is no absolute measure of wilderness, then how can one claim to cover all aspects of the indefinable? Instead, a number of regions, some quite large others rather small, have been selected, and an attempt has been made to analyse their own special, unique characteristics. I shall be looking at the physical reality of a place and the no less important, though constantly changing, nature of man's place in that particular picture. At the heart of the descriptions lie a series of walks made at different times throughout the year: walks, because if you wish to assess man's place in a landscape, then you need to move at man's pace, and also, of course, because a good deal of the pleasure we take in the wilderness comes from the physical activity of walking. But this is not a book of walks – there is no intention to suggest that the routes I followed are the best or are even worth following at all. They happened to suit me.

And it would be to work against the whole concept of freedom, which is such a potent force in the appeal of the wild, to attempt to define too closely pathways and directions.

I have to record that in the course of working on this book, my own attitudes changed. My first idea had been to think in terms of a series of long, demanding walks, days of steady striding, carving up the land into measured miles. There is an undeniable pleasure in the physical exhilaration of the long walk, a satisfaction in reaching some distant goal, in overcoming weather, fatigue and blisters. But then I began to feel that this impulse to push onwards was becoming the end rather than the means to the end. I began to take my time, to stop and look or simply to sit and wait for a particular place to make itself known. Ideally, one gets to know a region through familiarity, by seeing it in all seasons and all weathers, experiencing all its moods. Alas, for those of us with a living to earn, this means going everywhere and seeing nothing. I shall continue to enjoy the special exhilaration of, say, the Three Peaks walk, but I am slowly learning patience. In the accounts that follow, I have looked at a few special places in an attempt to suggest something of the riches that may be found by those who take the time to look.

These are personal views of the landscape, and they are accompanied by a set of equally personal views, those of the photographer, Jorge Lewinski. His photographs are not meant to be mere illustrations of the text but are an expression of his own vision and reaction to Wilderness Britain.

1. OTMOOR

We are accustomed to thinking of the wilderness in terms of special places, tracts of land to which we make journeys of exploration. The majority of places described in this book fall within that category, but here we have an exception. It is an area which I might describe as a personal wilderness, not in the sense that I have any rights over it, but because it is a local wilderness within the terms of my everyday life. Many of us have such places, which can exist even in the centre of a major city – they are places we can turn to for a little solitude, places where we can step outside daily routines and the pressures of a working life. I was fortunate. For many years I had a lovely small-scale wilderness virtually on my doorstep. It may not, however, be there for ever, but that is a subject which will emerge later in the story of this small patch of wild country, Otmoor.

Every morning when I got out of bed and pulled back the bedroom curtains I used to look out over a wonderful wide expanse of land. It was never the same from one day to the next. My favourite days were those on which banks of white cumulus piled up and set off on a steady drift across the blue sky, moving in procession above the rising ground of Brill hill, a dark, uneven line. It defined the far horizon which on a clear day is punctuated by the spiky outlines of trees and blobs of houses. And between myself and this cloud-dominated horizon lay a wide, flat expanse of greenery, stretching away out of my line of vision. Although I could see only a fraction of Otmoor, I was very aware of this flat land which spaced out the hills beyond, for it was the land which filled the gap between the horizon and home. And it is a very odd, very distinctive tract of land, which like so much of Britain has changed its character time after time through long periods of history, through eras recorded in books and annals and back still further to the time where the only records lie in the land itself. I am reminded again of the extraordinary changes that this country has undergone through the ages by a piece of rock picked up in a walk across the moor. It is a piece of stone, a conglomerate, small enough to sit comfortably in the palm of my hand, and embedded within the lump is a whole colony of sea shells – mussels, winkles, tiny scallops and the remains of oysters. So here I sit, as near to the centre of England as makes no odds, looking over what was once the sea. Change here is measured on a scale so large that it has no real significance in terms of human lives. Yet that self-same tract of land has gone through changes almost as dramatic as that from seashore to moor in a period covered by a few generations. My little local moor may be a puny thing compared to some of the great tracts but it is not insignificant – and it is certainly not lacking in interest.

Otmoor is ringed by seven villages, which though small are always known as the Otmoor Towns. The occupants of these towns once held rights in the common land, while the rights to fowling and fishing were held by the Lords of Beckley. So the moor remained for centuries as a generally waterlogged wasteland, drained, in so far as it was drained at all, by the River Ray. It was a huge bog, sitting on the top of a 450-ft-deep layer of clay. A few sheep grazed there, but were likely to be afflicted by various forms of foot-rot, and the principal inhabitants were flocks of geese. In winter it was little better than a shallow lake, and was then of little or no use to anyone. Yet the moor was important to the community for summer grazing and it provided reed and sedge to thatch the village cottages. Then came the Age of Improvement. Eighteenth-century Britain saw a great movement towards the enclosure of the old common lands, so that better and more efficient use could be made of them. But the ordinary folk were inclined to ask questions such as 'better for whom?' and seldom found the answers acceptable.

In 1815 Parliament decreed that Otmoor should be enclosed. Work began slowly on altering and canalizing the course of the River Ray

Looking across Otmoor to the rising ground of Beckley.

and drainage ditches were cut. There were endless arguments about the whole affair, and when the arguments finished, the real troubles began. The villagers who had held allotments which they had been given in the past in lieu of their rights to the common, were told they must pay their share of the drainage costs or give up their land. This was no choice at all, for few of them had any money to pay for anything beyond the necessities of life. And when the new work, which was supposed to herald a new age of prosperity, was completed, it proved to be less than satisfactory. The bank constraining the Ray and forcing it into its new channel gave way and resulted in widespread flooding. Discontent also overflowed into action, and the years of the Otmoor Riots began. Embankments were cut, hedges and fences pulled down and buildings destroyed. The troops were called in and even managed arrests. In September 1830 a group of Otmoor men were taken by wagon to Oxford Gaol, but on the way they had to pass through the big annual fair in St Giles. In the bustle and confusion every one of the prisoners escaped. It was 1834 before the troubles died down, but the resentment lingered, expressed in a verse of the time:

> The fault is great in Man or Woman
> Who steals the Goose from off a Common;
> But who can plead that man's excuse
> Who steals the Common from the Goose?

The drainage was improved, and the waste divided into a chequerboard of wide, flat fields. It was this view of the moor from the hill of Beckley that gave Lewis Carroll the landscape for *Through the Looking Glass.* Early in the book, Alice looks down from a little hill, much like that at Beckley:

For some minutes Alice stood without speaking, looking out in all directions over the country – and a most curious country it was. There were a number of tiny little brooks running straight across it from side to side, and the ground between was divided up into squares by a number of little green hedges, that reached from brook to brook.
  'I declare it's marked out just like a large chessboard!' Alice said at last.

And so it remains, and the view from Beckley hill is still much as Carroll saw it, and Alice's description is still apt. So, over the centuries this small tract of waste in the centre of Oxfordshire has changed its character to a quite remarkable degree, and the changes and the layers of changes are still there to be seen on the land today.

Thinking of the land that lies at your own doorstep is never quite the same as considering land, however well known, visited only on holidays. Where you can conjure up a memory of a special day on the

Lakeland fells, the local place is too familiar, has been seen in too many
moods, for any one image to fit. You see it in all weathers and all
seasons. In winter it frequently disappears from view altogether under
thick fog. In that season it is still much afflicted by floods – though not
to the extent that it was fifty years ago when it is recorded that it was
not unknown for people to skate across the entire breadth of the
flooded and frozen moor. It can still have its moments, however, when
the drainage waters prove too much for the Ray and locals have to
contemplate a dire threat to their social life as the waters rise and
threaten to cut them off from the village local. So I have seen the moor
in fine weather and wet, in flood and in the dry. I have seen the
passing seasons on the large scale, and day-to-day variations on the
small scale. One day the moor was softened in a thin haze, on another
the greens shine out like a paint-shop shade card. Any one description
seems inadequate, so what follows is simply a fragment out of a
continuous spectrum developed over the years that I lived on the edge
of Otmoor. This is just one walk on one day – not even much of a walk
by many standards, more a Sunday afternoon stroll.

My starting place was Oddington, a corruption of Otta's dun or
Otta's hill, presumably the same Otta who gave his name to the moor
itself. There was a monastery here in the twelfth century, but the
monks soon grew tired of paddling through the soggy land, and moved
to a higher and drier site at Thame. After that there were no more
excitements until the riots, and since then it has returned to its normal
tranquillity. A track leads off from the green, opposite the little
church, to cross the New River Ray. This is the straight, canalized
river, whose level is constantly going up and down in a most
extravagant manner – partly because of the effects of the weather, but
rather more because of artificial control through sluices. It is possible
to take a shallow draught boat on the river, from the weir that marks
the confluence with the Cherwell in Islip, along to Oddington and
across the moor. We used to have a family canoe and we would paddle
up this way, struggling through weed and low branches, but feeling as
solitary and isolated from civilization as if on an expedition up the
Amazon. Only the waterfowl keep you company, and the swans have
been known to express their disapproval of intruders. But if you can
cope with angry swans and the difficulties of the river, it is a fine way
to enjoy one aspect of Otmoor life.

To the walker, the river represents a moor boundary, for once
across it you are on Otmoor proper and can begin to appreciate its
very strange nature. It ought not to qualify as any sort of wilderness at
all, for much of Otmoor is cultivated in Alice's chessboard fields. Yet
you have no need to walk far onto the moor before you *feel* it as a
wilderness, which is what really matters. There is a quite extraordinary

feeling of solitude about the place, a feeling which is heightened the further you walk from the river. All around the edge of the moor the air is heavy with birdsong – twittering starlings providing the top line above the monotonous base of the wood pigeons. Yet on the moor, the song dies away. The little local guide to the moor lists nearly thirty regular visitors, but many of these are waterfowl on the river, and if the rest are around they keep remarkably quiet.

Walking out towards the centre of the moor on a footpath slightly raised above the surrounding fields you cross the straight lines of the drainage ditches, with a profusion of bulrushes and reeds marking their progress. The land is as flat as the fens, but the effect is very different, for the flatness is so circumscribed. On every side the low hills rise up: to the east, the tower of Islip church stands proud, matched in the north by the no less prominent tower at Charlton. To the west lies distant Brill, to the south Beckley and Noke, all on rising ground, all defining the limits of the little wilderness. It is a world that exists entirely within these set boundaries, and within these limits the changes wrought by man soon become apparent. The straight course of the New River is followed half a mile further on by the wriggling, much depleted course of the original river. It provides the one touch of asymmetry in this well-ruled landscape.

The fields might seem of themselves to be of little interest, but to the local historian they are a source of great fascination, for in their names, which have changed continuously over the years, you can trace the history of the land. Some are named after the owners, either as individuals – Tredwell's Field or Wise's Field – or office-holders – Parson's Ground. There are field names which tell of the nature of the land. The Fleets is a version of Flits or marshes, The Pill is an old name for a quaking bog. This is a good name to take note of, for when you reach the heart of the moor you discover just how appropriate it is. There are names which tell of uses – The Goosey, Osier Bed Ground. And one name takes us back even further, Roman Road Ground. The significance of the names may not always be obvious as you stroll through the fields, but by putting the name together with careful observation of the land, a pattern of use does begin to emerge.

At the centre of the moor two special aspects of the place become very clear. The field-name Roman Road Ground receives its justification, and the last of the truly wild moor, the moor of quaking bog, is found. The Roman road was part of a route from Bicester to Dorchester, and the Romans did precisely what Romans are always supposed to have done – headed straight for their objective, regardless of the obstacles that sat across their track. The line can be seen now as a raised path, though for much of its length it is notoriously wet and boggy, which must have made it a nuisance from the beginning as far as travellers were concerned. There is not a great deal now to distinguish it from the other straight tracks across Otmoor, though archæologists are hoping to find evidence of bridge-building where it crosses the Ray between Fencott and Merton. There is, however, one object in the centre of the moor which tradition has it was connected with the old road – Joseph's Stone.

Precisely what Joseph's Stone may be is a subject of some debate. Some hold that it is a Roman milestone, others a Roman surveyor's mark, while still other experts claim it is of far later date, an early mounting-block for riders. There is some evidence to support the latter view, since it is shown in an early nineteenth-century drawing bearing the inscription:

> Joseph Guilder brought this stone
> To help people up when they were down.

This does not, of course, preclude the stone from having a history that predates Mr Guilder's arrival on the scene. Such a wealth of speculation might seem excessive for one stone, and broken at that. Yet the interest it arouses is so great simply because Otmoor as a whole seems so bereft of landmarks. The flat land spreads out in all directions, only slightly disturbed by the minor surface upheavals that mark the drainage ditches.

Away from the stone and the line of the Roman road, the old moor still exists. There is not much of it, true, but it still seems a minor miracle that any really wild land does exist at all in this part of the country. To the casual visitor it might seem little more than a squelching area in the heart of a dull land of flat fields. To many others it is the last remnant of the old land. Botanists cherish it, for it is home to rare species, and even those who would be hard put to it to distinguish between the daisy and the dandelion, can enjoy the list of Otmoor plant names which is so splendid they might then even feel moved to set out to add physical reality to those names. The admirable local guide by M. G. Hobson and K. L. H. Price, which is a fund of information on Otmoor, lists all the plants, with full Latin tags and their fascinating popular names. Who could resist searching for the different members of the orchis family – the early purple orchis, the green-winged orchis or the butterfly orchis – or perhaps, less exotically, the marsh violet and the red goosefoot. Others, alas, sound less enticing to the uninitiated. Bladderwort sounds like a painful disease and frog-bit suggests dissection lessons in the school lab. For those well versed in the intricacies of the botanical world all are no doubt of equal interest, but for those who are too busy, or more likely too idle, to acquire a real knowledge of plant life, the names remain to be savoured. And the plants become brief flashes of colour to be enjoyed for themselves without the benefit of proper nomenclature.

From this point at the centre of the moor you can choose any point of the compass to continue the walk – east towards Horton-cum-Studley and so off the moor, north to Fencott, west the way you have come, or south towards Beckley, where other tracks lead round a wide circuit, some four miles back to Oddington. It was the latter route that I took, south across more of the complex of drainage channels, before striking off westwards towards Noke. Looking at the level land of the moor, you might reasonably expect the going to be so easy as scarcely to be worth the trouble. But if the area is little visited by walkers, it is very popular with riders. Horses churn up the paths and bridleways, and suddenly the walk can seem to be surprisingly hard work. Not that I am in any position to complain, since my daughter's horse has added its share to the quagmire, and it really is a magnificent spot for a gallop. In fact, as you pick your boots out of yet another cloying patch of clay, you begin to think that riding is a far more satisfactory means of covering the moor than walking.

As the track swings away from the direction of Noke to follow yet another ditch-side embankment, the pattern of the walk becomes clear. You walk along a ridge, formed from the material excavated when the ditch was first dug. And it is this excavated material, thrown up out of the ditch, which provides the clearest indication of the distant origins of the land. Here is the evidence of the marine life of past ages, including some massive oyster shells. With all the Lewis Carroll connections with the area, you cannot help wondering if perhaps the walrus and the carpenter came further inland than is generally believed. The nearer you get to Noke, the more the nature of the country changes, as the moor and the surrounding country meet at a very distinct boundary. A thickset spinney points out from the hill, jabbing a finger into the moor, but elsewhere village land and moor land keep themselves very much to themselves. At the boundary, the way eases until the path swings away again across the moor towards the Ray and Oddington. So the walk remains a bit of a slog to the end.

Those who regard the Three Peaks or the Snowdon Horseshoe as a moderate day's outing might perhaps look at our minuscule wilderness with disdain. It certainly offers no great physical challenge, but it does provide something which I regard as being at least as important: a very distinctive character. It is not just a small-scale version of some larger wilderness, but is complete within itself, with a unique atmosphere. And even if I were never able to walk across it again, I should always be glad of its presence, happy to know each morning that this particular piece of wild land is there.

Recently, however, it did seem that this might not continue for very much longer for the motorway planners turned their eyes on

The River Ray, much altered for land drainage.

Otmoor. The plans to take the M40 extension over the moor gave rise to the sort of controversy that has not been seen in the area since the enclosure and drainage plans were first mooted nearly two centuries ago. Such controversies always prove extremely troublesome, since so many special interests become involved. Botanists want to preserve the rare species of Otmoor; the horse fraternity, not to mention the far more numerous horse sorority, want to keep the rides open. Some householders worry about noise, while others are more concerned with property values. There are objectors who dislike all motorways, and those who would simply be happy to see it diverted to run past someone else's back doorstep. The pro-motorway lobby have two great advantages: they know they want a motorway and care very little where it goes, and they have cash. So a certain feeling of gloom and resignation soon becomes apparent within the ranks of the antis, the group which receives my instinctive support, for emotional responses tend to be instantaneous whatever the logic of the case. But where do the rights and wrongs lie? Are the issues as clearcut as they appear?

Let me start in the role of devil's advocate, or perhaps I should say, let me pull off my walking boots and head for the car. As a driver, I spend as much time as anyone cursing the local roads as I tootle along at the back of a convoy of lorries. And if I were a manufacturer I should doubtless have even greater cause for complaint about long delivery times and high transport costs. I could argue that those who want to wander off across the moor are a very small minority, as anyone who lives in the area can testify. In any case, they enjoy the luxury of walking only because commerce and industry have created the wealth that makes leisure possible. Such justifications are not insignificant, but neither are they particularly convincing. This is not the place to go into the minutiæ of the arguments for there is a more fundamental issue here, the importance of which extends beyond the local considerations.

I would say that the inconvenience of the private motorisst, such as myself is of negligible importance. The notion that the motorway is indispensable if we are to continue to produce the wealth on which, ultimately, the whole community depends is an argument of much more substance. But it is an argument that needs to be put into perspective. We need to ask – creation of wealth towards what end? If the creation of wealth can be achieved only at the expense of the wholesale destruction of the environment, is such wealth worth having? The answer is, to some extent, a subjective one. Many people, perhaps the majority, care little or nothing about what happens to a piece of ancient wasteland such as Otmoor. They are more concerned with acquiring the cash to buy more. More what? It scarcely matters. But whatever they want, it makes little difference to the overall

pattern of life whether they have their new videos, cars or whatever now or later. It does matter, however, if something irreplaceable is destroyed. In the modern world of increasing pressures, the need for the wilderness, however small it might be, has never been greater. And each time another piece is nibbled away it goes for ever.

This, it seems to me, is the crucial argument which applies not merely to my own small, local patch but to all our threatened wild places. Otmoor simply presents the whole problem in the sharp detail of a microcosm. I do believe that ultimately the quality of life in this land will depend on how we treat places such as this. It is a theme which will recur in different forms throughout these pages. In 1984 it seemed that the conservation battle had been won, that Otmoor had been spared the ravages of the motorway. But the Government report still left many questions unanswered. I should like to believe that this tiny wilderness, representative of so many other similar patches of precious land, will survive. But I have the sad, perhaps defeatist, feeling that the battle may have been won, but the war is not yet over. They are going to try to steal the common from the goose once more.

The distant tower of Charlton-on-Otmoor church seen across the moor.

2. BODMIN MOOR

Cornwall really is different, a separate entity, even if the differences which divide it off from the rest of Britain might not be immediately apparent. Sometimes those differences are first discerned in a chance remark that seems to be quite foreign, foreign that is to those of us who come from east of the Tamar. 'Just come across from England, have you?' asked the shopkeeper in Launceston, and sailing out of Falmouth a little later, it was the Cornish national flag that fluttered above the red sail. But such differences could easily be dismissed as the quirks of fashionable regionalism, were it not for the fact that there really is something more to Cornwall, something in the air and the land that sets it apart. The distinguishing factor does not thrust itself forwards; it insinuates itself gently and slowly into the sensibility.

As with so many others, my own introduction to Cornwall was to the Cornwall of the seaside – Atlantic rollers to be dived through, French cricket on the beach. Year after year, we brought the children to the same house in the village of St Mabyn, between Bodmin and Wadebridge. It was inland, away from the crowds but within a short drive of the sea and the beaches, which still seem after many excursions to other lands to be the best. How irritating it is to be told plonkingly, with that devastating, unconsidered honesty of the young, that some spot reached after much travel and at a good deal of expense is 'not as good as Cornwall'. St Mabyn seemed ideal for a family holiday, for the house itself was isolated and approached down a long drive fringed by a bamboo jungle that was all the wilderness a young child could want. It had everything from the ferociously loud rooks, harmless but as fierce of voice as a mountain-top full of golden eagles, to a colony of grass snakes, combining the pure pleasure of horror and fright with the minimum of actual danger. Excursions were, at first, mainly limited to outings to the sea – a drive along the high-banked lanes to the level sands and gentle waters of Rock or to the exhilaration of the Polzeath surf. Then there were mornings spent blackberrying in the lanes or meandering across the fields. And, as the children grew older, so the excursions and the walks lengthened, while at the same time that unique Cornish atmosphere was beginning to seep through into the consciousness.

The otherness of Cornwall now seems to me to emanate from the landscape itself and from its historical associations, but at first it seemed to come through growing intimacy with the people. The casual visitor will tell you, as all casual visitors always tell you everywhere, that the locals are 'only out for your money'. Considering that tens of thousands descend on the region every summer demanding to be entertained and amused, it would not be too surprising if this were the case. 'The English', after all, show little enough interest in the region and its problems for the rest of the year.

The road from Camelford leading off towards Rough Tor and Brown Willy.

In fact the relationship is not, and never could be, as simple as that. It is true that the Cornish are out to make money from tourism, for there seems to be little else left as the traditional industries of mining, quarrying and fishing have steadily declined, yet at the same time there is a growing feeling that tourism must not be allowed to encroach too far on a peculiarly Cornish way of life. It might seem to the outsider that efforts to restore old customs and the ancient Cornish language are meaningless exercises in archaism, but they are also symbols of a desire to keep an identity preserved in spite of the demands of the visitors. And in conversation over the evening pint one becomes increasingly aware that many of the Cornish are very much concerned to establish their status as members of the Celtic race. It is that Celtic history that has left a unique mark on the land.

Those who never travel beyond the beaches will never see this other – natives would argue, the real – Cornwall. In my case it was the steadily lengthening walks away from our base that made me increasingly aware of the marks of history, and not merely of the ancient past, but also the peculiarly Cornish recent past as well. You soon find the evidence of an ancient culture in the strange standing stones – the quoits, the stone circles and groups as mysterious as Men-an-Tol, the Devil's Eye, which includes an enormous, vertical stone ring. And, of a later date, there are the quintessential symbols of the more recent past – the ruins of the mine engine-houses with their exclamation-mark chimneys punctuating the skyline. I began hunting down these remnants of the past, each so very different in character. The ancient stones, their true significance now largely lost, are surrounded by mystery and legend. The engine-houses are romanticized, rather than romantic, ruins, for in spite of all the Poldarking laid over them in the interests of tourism they really belong to a severely practical world of hard work and endeavour. These two sets of monuments, poles apart, define the extremities of the Cornish past. They have nothing to do with the saucy postcard world of Newquay or the 'quaintness' of St Ives. They represent the other Cornwall, much of which remains untouched by tourism, but not untouched by history. They speak of the old Cornwall, and that presence is felt nowhere more strongly than on Bodmin Moor.

Bodmin Moor has somehow missed out on the publicity that surrounds the other moors of the south-west. Exmoor is Lorna Doone country, Dartmoor the home of the Hound of the Baskervilles, the 'great Grimpen Mire' and convicts in arrowed suits breaking stones. No one mentions Bodmin, yet it covers a vast area and is no less fascinating than its more famous neighbours – and a good deal less visited. Today, however, it is carved into halves by the A30 road. When we first visited Cornwall in the days before motorways, this was an area that scarcely registered at all, merely another landmark to tick off on the long journey which had included the notorious horrors of the Exeter by-pass. Today the traffic streams through, though a good many will pause at the romantically named Jamaica Inn. Whatever memories of smugglers and dark deeds the place may contain must long since have been dispelled, yet this for many remains the sole encounter with the moor. The motorist who turns south will at least get a feel of the real moorland and a glimpse of the Celtic past, for here the first half of the land of legend begins. And if the legend has perhaps as little basis in historical fact as the wilder stories of highwaymen and smugglers, at least its physical manifestation has something very real to offer. My own explorations of Bodmin began in this southern section and it was here that I returned to find, to my great delight, that little if anything had changed in the years that had passed since we first set out in family crocodile to explore the moor.

My new base for exploration was St Neot, one of those typically clenched-up villages squashed into a fold between the hills, a tough little granite cluster of houses. I visited the village in late May when Cornwall is at its loveliest. The crowds had not yet gathered, and the banks that close in the narrow lanes were awash with colour, laid on from a rich palette of flowers, dominated by the crimson of wild fuchsia. That the settlement is an ancient one can be seen in the Dark Age crosses though, as so often in Cornwall, the church also exemplifies the complexity of Cornish history. Oak Apple Day sees a curious ceremony, when a small tree is laboriously raised to the top of the church tower where it will remain for a year until it is, in turn, replaced. The ceremony tells of another Cornwall, the one that has strong ties with the land across the Tamar. But idiosyncrasies can be of more modern origin, and the churchyard boasts a new sundial of mind-boggling complexity. Perhaps it is just a sign that the ingenuity of the Cornish, the men who more than any others were responsible for bringing in the age of the steam engine, is still present. There is, however, a certain wistfulness about St Neot. Like many of the settlements clustered around the edge of the moor, it owed its prosperity to the wealth beneath the ground, in this case the local slate mines. The industry has died, leaving the caverns as just another tourist attraction. But Cornwall in May is seldom a time when thoughts turn to underground exploration, especially when the birds are singing, the sun shining and the moors that rise up above the houses look their most inviting.

Bodmin Moor represents the highest point in Cornwall, though it seldom rises above a thousand feet. It is a mixture of high plateau and low-lying, often marshy, ground, which makes the selection of routes a matter that deserves some care. There are a few granite peaks, poking their heads above the surface, notably Rough Tor and Brown Willy to the north, but an energetic walker could traverse the entire moor, taking in all the high points, on a single day's outing. Such an expedition is possible, but not necessarily the best way to get to know the place. There are tracts of country where it really does seem that the main pleasure lies in the exhilaration of a long, upland walk and the steady unrolling of fresh horizons. Bodmin Moor does not fit that category. The distances are not quite sufficient to give the satisfaction of tired achievement that marks the end of a really long walk. And the A30 presents an unwelcome interruption to the rhythm of the day, a noisy, oily intrusion into an otherwise peaceful landscape. Then again, the moor has so much to offer, so many intriguing details to explore, so many questions to be answered that the planned long walk can easily become a short walk, as the day slides by in localized inquisitiveness. I have attempted long walks in the past, but never quite achieved them, so on this occasion I bowed in advance to what would certainly prove necessity and settled for local explorations of the moor; dividing it into the areas north and south of the main road.

I have never been greatly addicted to walking along public roads,

The path across Lower Moor to Rough Tor.

but have always been prepared to make an exception in Cornwall. The narrow, minor roads, trench-like between their banks, offer a wonderful seclusion which out of the holiday season can be blissfully peaceful. There can, however, be disadvantages at any time. The summer tourist tends to regard the narrow, blind lanes with acute suspicion, driving slowly and cautiously with much sounding of the horn. The locals are less circumspect, and a certain fatalism can be observed among the older inhabitants who take a remarkably cavalier attitude towards fellow road-users. This is merely an extension of an old Cornish tradition that treats mechanical transport as a servant, not a master, disposable because replaceable. It was after all that great Cornish genius, Richard Trevithick, who, after the first successful trial with his newly invented steam car, left it to simmer while he celebrated at a local inn. Simmering turned to boiling, pressure mounted and the machine exploded. Trevithick, it is said, showed little concern. Few cars can be heard exploding in Cornwall these days, but many are treated with little respect – or so it seems to the walker trapped between the high grass verges as he sees some ancient vehicle all but bouncing from bank to bank as it weaves towards him. I remember one elderly lady who was notorious throughout the district

'The Cornish Alps': white mountains of spoil from the china clay quarries.

and who peered out at the world myopically through the densest of lenses, the thickness of which was not, alas, sufficient to compensate for failing eyesight. She kept on course only by using the banks as if they were meant as tram tracks. The only defence if caught in a narrow section was to leap up the bank and hang on to anything that looked likely to take your weight. The old lady generally passed on oblivious of the terror she had left behind her. Such are the hazards of the Cornish lane, and though the attractions are there in sweet-smelling honeysuckle and fuchsia, it is always pleasant to turn off onto the footpath up the moor.

The true starting-point of this excursion was to be Crow's Nest, a hamlet on the southern edge of Caradon Hill. On this southern part of the moor you have the curious experience of being surrounded by the works of man, while at the same time seeming to be in remote and unspoiled country. For this is the heart of a once busy mining area, where men went deep below the surface for copper and tin. This is one of the vital elements, not only in the story of the moor, but in the story of Cornwall as a whole. Now that the miners have left, all that they made is slowly and inexorably returning to its origins. As one cannot ignore the physical remains of man's intrusion into this landscape, since to attempt to do so would be to misread the land that one now sees, I decided to use them. The route I chose to follow was that of the early railway or tramroad that served the mines and quarries of the moor. These were not railways as we think of them today with fast locomotives, but railways where the work was done by horses. My notion was to try to follow the route round Caradon Hill to the Cheesewring and on to Twelve Men's Moor or wherever else it would lead me − for, truth to tell, I was not altogether certain of the line. There were indications of the old line on the Ordnance Survey map, but they were not always clear and, to make matters worse, there often seemed to be a multiplicity of routes. It might seem perverse to hunt out a wilderness via a railway line, but these old decayed lines have much to say for themselves. If in your mind you can go back a century and a half to the time when the engineers came to this lonely moor, and try to see it through their eyes, then the land begins to take on a quite different significance. This is not the grandest of moors perhaps, but look at it as a location for building a railway and the hills seem to grow in front of your eyes, until they seem as awesome as the highest range of mountains.

The early track is easily identified, swinging up the hill towards a prominent group of engine-houses. In recent years, the Cornish engine-house has become as much a visual cliché as a symbol, its distinctive outline appearing on book-jackets, brochures and even tea-towels. Seen close to, however, they become something more than a cliché. When they were built, they stood surrounded by a jumble of other buildings which, at the vast majority of deserted mines, have simply crumbled away. But the engine-houses are a different proposition, made of sterner stuff, for they were built to withstand the action of giants, the plunging shocks and rocking beams of the mighty steam-engines. Yet the engine-house remains a potent symbol, a symbol of an underground world that it served, a dark labyrinth beneath the moor. In the nineteenth century more than 200,000 tons of ore were taken from this group of mines on Caradon Hill. Now all that is left is the spoil spilling down the hill from the gaunt ruins, and the track of the railway beneath the collapsed arch of a bridge. There is a true majesty in these ruins, the majesty of great endeavour. The mines have long since been silenced, and beneath your feet the other world is collapsing, as galleries cave in, shafts crumble. At the surface, too, the buildings are crumbling, the granite that was taken from the earth is falling back to the earth. Vegetation grows through and over the ruins, and the traces slowly disappear as the wilderness reasserts its power over the best efforts of man.

Following the old track provides a pleasant and comfortable pathway around the flank of the hill, a pleasant walk on a day of pale spring sunshine. The route then runs across a minor road to yet more mines and engine-houses, which provide an interesting contrast – Phoenix United, the mightiest of them all, and its more modest neighbour which was temporarily converted into a dwelling-house. This was a short-lived experiment, and all that remains now is an incongruous domestic chimneypot, a memory of someone's dream to have an unusual home on the moor. But even in terms of the purely human history of Bodmin Moor, the engine-houses are Johnny-come-latelies, for a little to the west on the flat, windy plane beneath the hill stand three stone circles. Like all their mysterious brethren these have yet to be explained by modern man. There are, of course, no end of explanations, varying from the sensible to the absurd. But as no one explanation appears to offer any more supporting evidence than the next, you may choose as you please among them – or simply walk away, content to leave the mystery with the stones.

As the track leads northwards, so the scenery becomes steadily more rugged, the works of man less and less obtrusive. The signs are still there, however, if you know what to look for. Along the track leading up the hill you can see parallel rows of stones with holes in the middle of each block. These are stone sleepers to which the rails were once spiked. They lead round to the quarry of the Cheesewring where shattered stones form grotesque statuary round the slopes. But, however fantastical these artificially created forms might be, they cannot compare with those of the Cheesewring itself. Here, at one of

The steep, verdant banks of a Cornish lane near St Neot.

the high points of the moor, one can scramble up over these eroded blocks of granite, which do indeed resemble a pile of balanced cheeses, and from the top survey the moor stretching out in steady rise and fall before you. It seemed an empty land, but it had none of that rather brooding melancholy which can sometimes afflict moorland, for the bright sunlight was picking up the first, fresh greening of spring. Sometimes this can be an illusion, those bright spots in the hollow indicating nothing more enticing than the squelch and cloying mud of a marsh. It seems as if the moor goes on for ever until it reaches the coast: it will not in fact ever get that far. The old rail track continues to lead northwards towards Kilmar Tor.

Now the moorland seems empty indeed, the track becomes increasingly difficult to locate, and map and compass are more useful than signs on the ground. You follow the track as best you can, and then even the faint traces disappear. It has vanished, come to a full stop. But it has already done its job, having brought you to the heart of the moor. It has taken you from the Bodmin of mines and quarries to an older Bodmin, where the physical remains now are of the old hut circles, the first human settlements on the moor. The track has also brought you to the Bodmin of legend. Ahead is a ridge known as King Arthur's Bed, and of all the stories that have lingered round this region it is the Arthurian legend that has proved the most tenacious. The prosaic may argue that it is doubtful whether Arthur was a historical character at all and will claim, rather more convincingly, that even if he did exist in the world of men he is unlikely to have had a great deal to do with Bodmin Moor. Certainly, looking around this empty land, it is hard to people it in imagination with the chivalrous knights of the round table. But such visions represent only the outward trappings of the stories. At their core is a hunt for purity and virtue in a world where such commodities are rare. The legends deal with mysteries that lie beyond physical reality. Some people hold strong beliefs about the presence of strange forces that refer back to the time of Arthur. Alas, I am not one of them. Arthur's Bed is just a name attached to a patch of rising ground. I knew I was standing at the end of a disused railway, but that was pointed towards Camelford not Camelot. I turned for home, but later I returned to the moor to a point further west where perhaps, I thought, the spirit of legend might still linger.

Dozmary Pool is said to be the lake where Excalibur was returned to the waters. Tennyson in his *Morte d'Arthur* described the mere 'and the long ripple washing in the reeds'. The long ripple still washes the reeds of the dark pool, and if you sit by its side at sunset you may perhaps imagine that scene in the words given to Sir Bedivere:

Then with both hands I flung him, wheeling him;
But when I looked again, behold an arm,
Clothed in white samite, mystic, wonderful,
That caught him by the hilt, and brandish'd him
Three times, and drew him under in the mere.

I am afraid I seem to lack the kind of imagination that can re-create such scenes in the mind, but this has never troubled me. The dark lake, the dry swish of reed and the pale ripple of the waters were quite enough by themselves. They needed no embellishments to augment their own mystery and tranquillity. I went back again inland to find more of the moor itself, and left the legends down by the pool. The Arthurian names do recur on the northern part of the moor, with King Arthur's Hall set in the middle of his Downs, but these are so obviously names of mere whimsy that they scarcely register. In fact, when one turns to the northern moor, thoughts of man's place in the scheme of things hardly occur at all. Only the remnants of hut circles, barely recognizable to any but the expert eye, serve as reminders that man has always come to terms with this wild upland.

The simplest approach to the highest points of the moor is via the Jubilee Drive from Camelford, a grandiose name suggesting a triumphal procession which happily never materializes. Instead a typical up-and-down lane leads out past Rough Tor farm to a car park, from where a bridge leads across a small stream and the pathway can then be followed to the top of the hill. A steady and undemanding ascent, the path takes you past the spot where the clearest evidence of the early settlement can be seen. The hut circles are surrounded by the remnants of the old field system, the lynchets terraced out of the hillside. Having just left a fertile and comparatively level valley it seems a mystery, as one scrambles up among the rocks to the rough, jagged outline of the summit, why anyone should choose to farm up here in the first place. The tough, spiky grass and heather of the moor look well enough, but even the most vivid imagination would have difficulty in conjuring up images of grain growing amid the wind-tossed grass. The problem lies largely in our inability to see the land as our ancestors saw it. We forget, as we look down at the land gently shelving away from the moor to the sea, that thousands of years of forest clearance have gone into the making of such a scene. We do not see the tangle of trees and undergrowth that faced our ancestors as they turned their steps uphill to scrape at the soil with primitive ploughs and dig out the stones to build their shelters.

The weather this day was on the change. The wind sharpened from the west, and in the distance the clouds gathered. White became tinged with grey, in places fraying to allow a dark slant of rain to join clouds to earth. But the day was warm, and the thought of the occasional shower by no means unpleasant. We had reached the top of Rough Tor and could easily have turned back and kept dry, but one of those imperatives was at work that afflicts walkers – or at least this walker. It is always satisfying to rest awhile on the top of a hill viewing the world around, seeing the changing patterns on the cloud-shadowed land. Yet somehow the pleasure is diminished by the nagging thought that the hill you can see just a couple of miles away is higher than the one you are occupying. True in this case: the map gave the difference as a mere 66 feet, but somehow that extra height demands your presence. It was simply too near at hand to be ignored.

Brown Willy lies to the south of Rough Tor, separated from it by a stream and some notably boggy ground. The route down is through the hut circles of the southern slope, after which it is a case of selecting not so much the quickest as the driest route. Green is a good measure of damp. It may look more inviting than the sombre colours of the moor, but if you wish to avoid the heavy going, plodding

St Neot and the edges of the moor.

through ground that seems intent on sucking the boots from your feet, then you would be well advised to settle for the duller colours. In practice the way proves simple and the stream can be crossed with ease half-way along the length of the hill. From here it is possible to walk up through yet more hut circles – though here not as well defined as on Rough Tor, to the new summit. Here you can stand feeling that you have finally reached the real heart of the moor, the centre of a true wilderness. But then you find that you can just hear the noise of traffic on the road to the south, an unwelcome intrusion, as irritating as the whine of an insect just after you have put out the bedroom light. There was little encouragement to linger, for the clouds were now with us, and the view was steadily shrinking as the light rain swept in.

The pleasantest return route is to turn north where Brown Willy comes down via a long, gently humped ridge to the flat land of Davidstow Moor, skirting two marshes. Indeed the land at the foot of the hill is so unexpectedly flat for such a region that it harboured an airfield, most of which has now disappeared under forestry plantation. Each in their way marks yet another stage in man's adaptation of the land. The airfield is already little more than a vague memory, broad pathways now where there were runways, and all, no doubt, soon to be quite lost in the spreading woodland. Now there is only a short walk left across a low hill to complete the journey back to Camelford.

There are always those who tend to undervalue Bodmin, regarding it as little more than a second-class Dartmoor. Certainly it covers a smaller area and its peaks are lower while, since it shares the same geological formation, much of the landscape is very reminiscent of the Devon neighbour. Nevertheless, Bodmin Moor seems to me to have a quite different character, one which is neither quickly nor easily grasped. Over the years I have explored it in detail, in a way which I have never explored Dartmoor, nibbling away at it, rather than taking it in big bites. No doubt this reflects a personal interest in the mining history of the region, as much as its appeal as a place of wildness and loneliness. Yet I have, time after time, been impressed by the special beauty of the place. The works of the miners and others who came to make their livelihoods here have already completed much of their journey back to a seemingly natural state. The stones of the engine-houses are the stones of the moor, and the deserted buildings can seem to hold as natural a place in the landscape as the loneliest crag. It is perhaps a feeling of great things done but great things ended that provides a uniquely melancholy note to the Bodmin theme. Coming here, even immediately after a visit to Dartmoor, produces no sense of anticlimax, but rather heightens the sense of difference, helps to bring out the special characteristics that make Bodmin Moor unique.

3. DARTMOOR

Houndtor Wood on the eastern edge of Dartmoor.

Saddle Tor, north of Ashburton.

Everyone it seems wants a piece of Dartmoor. The military wish to practise on it, firing their guns at nothing in particular, and if their presence on the moor is not always apparent to the casual visitor, then it is all too clear to anyone taking out the map to plan a walk in the area. The northern moor is liberally bespattered with the ominous words 'Danger Area', suggesting that a walk in that region might be as comfortable as a wander through a minefield. In fact the firing ranges are not quite the problem that they appear to be. Vying with the military, however, for use of the moor are the farmers who are regarded by some who wish to preserve the 'essential character' of Dartmoor as a threat and a menace. This is a feature of the region of which it is impossible to be unaware, for slowly but steadily wilderness Dartmoor is disappearing under the plough. The moorland boundary is shrinking inwards before the invaders. Walkers and conservationists have no doubts about where the rights of the matter lie – but then neither do the farmers. Seen from the point of view of either protagonist, the issue seems clear. But is it in fact as obvious as it appears?

There is a large and articulate body of opinion among those who turn to the countryside for pure pleasure, which regards all farmers as

enemies and destroyers. They see farmers ploughing across footpaths, destroying rights of way. They record the destruction of ancient hedgerows and the demolition of mellow stone walls in favour of cheap, easily maintained – but oh so ugly – wire fencing. And they see farmers produce conditions around their properties which would never be tolerated in urban areas: motorcars are dumped and left to rot; corrugated iron sheds are put up that screech out their incongruity in the surrounding landscape. All these charges are made and, all too often, proved. And because this is so, too many fail to see that this is far from true of all farmers – and they fail to see that the issues are not as simple as they appear to someone who spends most of the year behind a desk. For many of those who complain are at best part-time countrymen and, of those who do live in country districts, few actually earn a living on the land. It is too easy to come to Dartmoor for a fine day's walking and bemoan what is happening to the land. We have all done it and, no doubt, will do it again. But it is worth pausing to look at the problem from the other side.

In 1979 I came to stay in the village of Sticklepath on the northern edge of the moor. On this occasion I was there to film an old water-powered forge, one of the many different small industries that once ringed Dartmoor – but that is another story. During the stay we put up at an old farmhouse, and I was so enchanted by the spot that I came back again shortly afterwards to use it as a centre for walking the northern moor. It was during that second stay that I learned something of the difficulties of forcing a living out of the fringe lands of the moor. What seems despoliation to some seems not just good husbandry and land reclamation to others, but the difference between economic survival and bankruptcy. On the farmer's side there is a tendency to see the walkers as fair-weather critics whose talk of preserving the essential nature of the land takes little account of the actualities of living and farming here for twelve months of the year. And the farmer often argues that his relationship to the land is in many ways more real than that of the walker who pays a weekend visit. The changes of weather and season have a significance for those who live on the land which the rest of us can never altogether come to understand.

The problem is not new, for the Dartmoor Preservation Society was founded a century ago in 1883, largely as a response to unauthorized and illegal enclosure of the common land. Such enclosures soon became accepted by common usage, whatever the legal situation might have been, and once accepted the situation proved irreversible. Regulations always seem to fail to meet the real needs of conservation, so that we find the Forestry Commission planting their regimented conifers in patterns which bear not the slightest resemblance to the underlying structure and character of the area. Government has always played a most ambivalent role in regions such as this. On the one hand they set up a National Park to protect the environment, while with the other hand they pass out grants to the farmers to aid them to fence it off, plough it up and close the pathways. So who are the heroes and who are the villains?

It is tempting to cast the government in the role of villain – any government of any persuasion – since we British are by nature slightly anarchic and anti-government at the best of times. And government certainly has been playing a ridiculous part in the proceedings, giving with one hand and taking with the other, leaving all parties in a state of confusion. Yet they are the one group which should be able to step aside from sectional interest and take a wider view. They have never been able to manage this in the past, and it seems most unlikely that they will have much greater success in the future, so that factions are left to get on with their squabbles. The truly sad thing is that there is not, in essence, so large a gap between the sides. The love which most farmers feel for the land is as great as anyone's, and if farming could only continue in the old way then everyone would be happy. But the farmer needs to be assured that he will not lose by the changes back to the earlier 'less efficient' methods. So why not subsidize such things as dry-stone walling and thatching to replace wire fencing and corrugated roofs. Why not spend cash where it matters if the landscape is to be preserved. Some, I know, throw up their hands in horror at such a suggestion, yet they are probably quite prepared to see millions spent on preserving some of the great landscape paintings by Constable or Gainsborough. If we can subsidize a representation of the landscape, why should we not subsidize the reality as well? After all, the worst that is likely to happen to the painting is that it will be sent off to another country. It will not cease to exist. Unless we take action quickly over the landscape, restoration will be impossible.

This is only a part of the threat facing wild Dartmoor. The military want more, the farmers want more – and the tourists want more. They want 'better access', and here perhaps lies the greatest threat of all, and here, too, the underlying arguments are surprisingly complex. Those who would argue, as I do, that the wilderness should be preserved as a wilderness or it is nothing, that increased access by motorcars can only destroy that which people believe they have come to see, must face up to the accusation of selfishness. Are we not trying to preserve the pleasures of the moor for the fit, the healthy and that minority – a small minority, we should admit – who are prepared to undergo fatigue and discomfort to discover the pleasures of the wild country for themselves? Yes, we are, but there is nothing to be ashamed at in this. It is a simple fact that the nature of the place makes it irreconcilable with the pressures of commercialism and the presence of the internal combustion engine. The thing is impossible. But what of all those people who crowd each summer onto the moor to play games, to picnic and to meander in the sunshine; what of their rights? Are they to be ignored? The answer is, yes, to some extent they must be if we are to preserve something precious for future generations. A wild place such as Dartmoor can only be destroyed, not created. We are the custodians, and if the name sounds pompous, then so be it.

Visit the most popular spots such as Postbridge in summer, and you will find crowds almost to rival those of Oxford Street during the January sales. And I do ask myself, sometimes, what they are getting out of it. The answer is, I suppose, fresh air, attractive scenery, and room for the kids to run around and have fun, and what's wrong with that? Or go to another popular beauty spot on the edge of the moor, Haytor, perhaps one of the most attractive and spectacular of the rock lumps heaved up into folds by volcanic action millennia ago. It looks, and is, an exotic formation, enticing any half-way adventurous child to

Haytor rocks.

scramble up the rough granite to stand in triumph on the summit. Visiting the region on a pleasant day in early spring, I did what everyone else did and took my moment of triumph on the summit of my miniature Everest. No one would wish to deny anyone this simple pleasure, and with the rocks so close to the road there will never be a shortage of visitors here. But clamber down the far side of the tor, turn away from the road and, quite suddenly, tranquillity returns. But very soon you find that the 'old Dartmoor' which we are so keen to preserve must once have been a good deal noisier, the air filled with sounds less harmonious than the laughter of children.

Beyond the rocks are the remains of Haytor Granite Tramway, a primitive form of railway used to carry stone from the local quarries. The name does not come from the stone that was carried but from the railway itself, for the rails are constructed out of granite blocks, cut to take waggon wheels. In a part of the world with no iron and a lot of stone, it made sense. It can be followed for miles, and comes complete with intersections, sidings and termini, while the sheer scale of the enterprise indicates just how busy this part of the moor must have been in the last century. Then the rattle of trucks, the crash of explosions, the ring of pickaxe on stone would have filled the air instead of the noise of people enjoying themselves, which we sensitive souls complain about so often. So which part of the past are we protecting – the past of empty moorland, or the past of sweating labourers hacking at stone that would go to build the commercial empires of the city? If a visit to Haytor does nothing else, it proves that there are no absolute rights and wrongs here.

Crowds are not a year-round problem on the moor, and in winter especially it provides such a daunting and hostile environment that few venture there apart from those whose livelihood demands that they should. It is possible to walk the moor in winter, but each year brings fresh evidence that it can be most foolhardy to do so. I chose early spring for a short visit of just a few days, in which I hoped to explore a little of what is perhaps the wildest land in England, if not in Wales and Scotland. For Dartmoor is vast, covering an area of some 200 square miles. It is so big that you would need to live there and walk it regularly if you wanted to claim anything more than a brief acquaintance. But even a short visit can reveal some of the essential character, and that great size does mean that anyone able and willing to make an effort can get away to find true solitude. This is particularly so if you start at the edge of the moor, rather than the centre.

Following the pattern of Bodmin, I took a nibble at the southern edge, and then a bite out of the north. The starting-point was the village of South Brent, typical of the small settlements that creep up to the edge of the moor and snuggle down in a protective fold, in this

Belsom Common,
north Dartmoor.

case the confines of the little Avon valley. The river itself pours down off the moor through a deep and very picturesque valley, thickly wooded in its upper slopes. Valleys such as this provide the only means by which natural woodland can penetrate onto the wild and windy spaces above. This river makes up in strenuous activity and variety for anything it might lack in terms of size and grandeur. It cascades over rocks to form deep, transparent pools, turned moody brown with peat. In spring the banks were freshened by the new leaves crowding each other for every available chink of light. There is something too of the harshness of the upland apparent, for the trees also compete for space, their boles engulfing and drooping over granite boulders, like double chins over a hard collar.

Shipley Bridge is a popular beauty spot, reached by steep, narrow lanes from South Brent. From here one can take a gentle stroll along the waterside to reservoirs higher on the moor. Alternatively you can strike up north onto Brent Moor, where very soon the true Dartmoor

Dartmoor ponies and Hound Tor.

asserts itself. Even on a fine spring morning it is not unusual to find you have the moor to yourself, in the sense that you can spend the day without meeting other parties of walkers. But you are certainly not alone in any other sense. On the lower slopes, sheep wander their own narrow pathways, heads down and nibbling while the new lambs teeter along behind. The young have their momentary fits of enthusiasm and energy, when they leap in the air, dash in circles, then stop as if to wait for applause. After that they are soon reminded that young lambs have other needs in life. Their anxious bleating is answered by the deeper note of the ewe and the little ones dash and bounce away to tug at the mother's teat, wagging their thick, heavy tails as they stoop for their feed. Brown, shaggy bullocks stare gloomily at distant horizons as they pause in their steady munching. Some stand in the centre of the track, eyeing the human visitors truculently, trying to stare them out. Then, at the last moment, they shamble away with a great air of grievance. Ponies mingle with the cattle, and a long-legged foal lollops awkwardly over the wiry turf.

The higher up the slope you walk, the fewer animals are met: but the birds are everywhere. There seems not to be a moment when the air is not full of their sound. An agitated skylark rises straight up from under foot, singing from the moment it leaves the ground. Grouse wait for the last minute before setting off like ground-skimming jets, zooming low over the surface with a furious whirr and rattle of wings. Spring is beautiful on the moor, a miraculous time of plenty and renewal, but it can also be hideously deceptive. Blue skies can vanish in a moment. The far distance appears in the sunlight as a shaded series of retreating hills, more like the cardboard cut-outs of a Victorian stage set than any reality. Each successive shape changes in tint with the retreating perspective. Then come the clouds and the sharp edges blur into an undifferentiated haze, and the swell of the moorland merges with the sky. Reference points are lost and the cosy landscape suddenly seems wild indeed – wild and a trifle alarming. Then the clouds part again, colours emerge from the darkness and the world is friendly once more. But the brief darkness acts as a warning that one should never underestimate the moor.

Bala Brook runs down the face of the moor in a deep cleft, surrounded by marshy, boggy ground – a part of the land which seems of no conceivable use to anyone. Yet embedded in the ground is a length of rusting iron rail, and further up the remains of a truck bogie. Why should anyone wish to build anything up here, let alone a railway? The answer is certainly not apparent to the casual gaze. While Bodmin has its traces of mining activities plainly on view, here, where the industrial activity was quite different, traces are a good deal more difficult to find and interpret. In fact, man has made good use of the moor in many ways: stone for building, peat for fuel and clay for the potter. Up here, what you are actually seeing are the traces of the Zeal Tor peat tramway, built in 1847 to carry peat down to Shipley Bridge, where naphtha oil was distilled out. It is perhaps an encouragement to environmentalists that so much activity has left so little trace that you need to be a detective to recognize the scant clues.

The top of the moor at over 1,500 feet is marked by a stone enclosure, and the route up runs past an even older monument. A single stone rears up by the track, a tall finger pointing skywards and known as St Peter's Cross. It is certainly not a Christian relic. It dates back far beyond that, and its significance can now only be guessed at. Once past the stone, it is no more than a short walk to the summit and a great panorama of moorland landscape. The sense of being alone in a great land is absolute and it is easy to believe that you have come not just to a wild land but to a completely natural landscape, where for once man has not left a mark. That delusion is shortlived. Two tracks lead down to the valley below Brent Moor. The more easterly crosses the stream in the valley bottom by means of a simple clapper bridge, a basic structure formed by piling up rocks to form piers on the stream bed and then laying slabs across the top of them. Such bridges are often spoken of as being very ancient, but there is no evidence to support that view, and opinion has now swung round to suggesting that they might be medieval or even more recent. It is rather a shame really that the experts have cast doubt on the old theory, for it would be pleasant to think that one was following an ancient track, particularly when it actually leads to a hut circle. How satisfying to the tidy mind if we were really crossing a bronze-age bridge to reach a bronze-age settlement. The second track leads to another hill, but one quite unlike any of the surrounding prominences. This one stands alone and symmetrically conical, a sure indication that its origins are probably not natural. And so it proves, for this is nothing more than a gigantic spoil heap.

It was time to retrace our steps, a notion encouraged by some decidedly ominous cloud build-ups. The forecasters had promised a good day, but had said that bad weather with heavy storms might be coming along later: there seemed to be a very good chance that they were coming sooner. In such circumstances, discretion is definitely to be recommended: the temperature can hurtle downwards as fast as the rain, and the walker finds progress getting ever slower with the increasingly heavy going. So the high part of the moor, Ryders Hill, was left for another day. The return was via the Avon reservoirs and an absolute jumble of old hut circles and enclosures that scatter across the hillside below the ridge of White Barrows and spread down into the Upper Avon valley. I find this a most difficult landscape to 'read' and understand, never being certain whether I am looking at an accidentally symmetrical arrangement of natural rock or the signs of an early settlement. These old settlements strain my comprehension in many ways. What must life have been like for a primitive people, armed with only the most rudimentary of tools, making a home in an environment which even now in spring was becoming more hostile by the minute? One can only speculate on the hardships they endured and the efforts they made to tame this fierce land. Speculation was, however, somewhat shortlived as the storm broke in the form of hail that slapped you painfully in the face. Head down, you lost interest in everything except the ground beneath your feet as you tugged the anorak hood further down and stomped gloomily on. The horizon vanished, visibility shrank to yards, and the only thing I could see at all clearly was a vision of a pint of Royal Oak on the pub bar. If ever I needed confirmation of the old advice about keeping a weather eye open, I got it at the end of that day's walk.

The northern edge of Dartmoor has quite a different character from that of the south. It is closely skirted by the main A30 road, yet for some reason never seems particularly crowded. The motorists, it

Belstone Common and the valley of the East Okement River.

seems, are generally on their way to somewhere else, to the beaches of Devon and Cornwall. Yet if anything, it is even more fascinating than the south, particularly for those who are as interested in the development of human settlement as they are in the natural scenery. As mentioned in the beginning of the chapter, I have developed a particular affection for the village of Sticklepath. It is not strictly a moorland village, perhaps, in the way that the more southerly villages can be, but it has always drawn its livelihood from the moor. The sheep that graze it were for centuries suppliers of raw material for local industry, for Sticklepath was a centre for the manufacture of woollen cloth. Wool was one factor in the equation: power was the other. At the western end of the village the river is dammed and its waters diverted into an artificial channel that runs along behind the houses. The water turned the wheels that drove the machinery of the mills, and waterwheels still turn to provide power for the great hammers and grindstone at Finch's Foundry. It was this that first brought me here, but it is the moor itself that brings me back.

From Sticklepath a pleasant lane leads up to Belstone and Belstone Common and what must surely be one of the loveliest spots in the whole region. The hamlet perches on its rounded hill, looking down on the deep cleft formed by the little river that meanders down, eventually to bring life and movement to the waterwheels of Sticklepath. From here one can turn towards a variety of tors, including the high point of aptly-named High Willhays (2,038 ft). But scattered across your path are those red-letter areas marked 'Danger', and even the notion of the frustration you would feel if you walked up there only to find you had arrived on the one day of the year when the moor was closed is so strong that it acts as a great disincentive. You can pick out routes through the area that would avoid the problem altogether, but the idea of coping with such artificial obstacles seems to make nonsense of the whole object of coming to Dartmoor. I come here for freedom, for a release from the petty restrictions of normal working life, so I have no wish to cope with them here. We strode off towards the more modest eminence of Cawsand Hill.

It is not a demanding walk, a gentle climb up a gentle slope, but if you have been stuck in the office for a good while and lack exercise, you soon know that you are climbing, and you can still enjoy a feeling of smug self-satisfaction at reaching the summit. On this occasion the smugness was slightly dissipated by finding a family party already there, including Granny, who looked as if she were ready for another twenty miles. She seemed to look at me slightly quizzically, as if wondering why I was sitting down for a rest on the summit cairn.

I took a route down the eastern slope towards South Tawton Common, aiming to cross on to Throwleigh Common on what promised to be a pleasant walk across gently undulating moor to end up at the hamlet of Wonson, adorned on the map by the tempting initials PH. The walk proved to be just what I had hoped, offering the quiet pleasures of the gentler moorland fringes and a rewarding pint at the end of the excursion. There were, however, other marks on the map. In the just legible squiggles of the Gothic script used by the Ordnance Survey to indicate antiquities, I could see the words 'Stone Row' written across the flank of Cawsand Hill. This was invitation enough for a minor detour. And there, sure enough, they were: parallel rows of stones stretching out down the hillside.

There is a genuine air of mystery about such phenomena. The moor was once populated by people about whose way of life we know very little. We do know, however, that although the simple struggle for existence must have absorbed most of their time and energy, they still found the time to quarry the stone and make these careful alignments among the rough tussocky grass of the hill. And we have no idea why. There are theories in plenty, and it just so happened that I had recently been sent a book on the subject of 'earth magic' to review. Trained as a scientist, I regard such matters with the deepest scepticism. I had also met a dowser at Sticklepath, and this is a subject where the evidence appears to be too strong for the whole thing to be dismissed out of hand. I even tried my hand at the art myself, with what appeared to be a certain degree of success. I would not put it any higher than that, for what I did could scarcely be described as a rigorous scientific experiment. The book had maintained that any dowser working with a pendulum in the presence of such stones would find bizarre things happening, so as I had some evidence that I could dowse and here were the stones, it seemed an irresistible invitation to a little experimentation. The nearest thing I could find to a pendulum was the compass on its neck cord but, feeling intensely stupid, I gave it a try. The improvised pendulum certainly seemed to show a strong tendency to move in circles rather than the approved straight line. Was this evidence of a strange power held in the stones which the ancients had been able to harness? If so, how was the power lost? Or was it evidence that when making such experiments you influence the result, however unconsciously, because it is much more interesting if the thing works? I am inclined towards the latter opinion. The mystery remains unresolved, just as the whole mystery of the stones remains. It is certainly a place which predisposes you to accept the presence of odd forces, for the stones themselves in such a remote spot create a special atmosphere. Yet the stones are small, the rows just one example among many on Dartmoor. They are as nothing compared with the greater stones and still greater mysteries to be found in other parts of the land.

Standing stones at Avebury.

The concept of wilderness is as much in the state of mind as it is in any objective reality. The native of the jungle is as familiar with the local intricacies of his own domain as the commuter in the London underground. Make them change places, and each would be as bemused as the other, feeling lost in some wild and menacing environment. One can be comfortable on a remote hilltop and menaced a mile from home. It is all a matter of surroundings, circumstances and individual attitudes. The regions we have already looked at have an air of wildness which is immediately felt even by the casual visitor. The area we are now turning to might seem to have little if any of these qualities, yet I would say that most people perceive a genuine wildness here, in the sense that they are confronted by circumstances where the normal responses of everyday life no longer seem appropriate. The wilderness may be felt in the conscious and subconscious mind, rather than in aching legs and sore feet, but it is none the less real for that. This does, however, mean that any

Marlborough Downs.

discussion of this particular brand of wilderness has to be in very personal terms, and in terms of a response which is particularly dependent on changes in circumstance and weather. But then such factors affect our judgement almost as much when we are looking at 'purely natural' phenomena.

I recall visiting the famous Niagara Falls many years ago. There is no denying that they are among the great natural wonders of the world, a mighty force of nature. They are also a four-star tourist attraction, so that the natural falls can be seen only against a totally unnatural background. Hotels and restaurants, souvenir shops and hamburger joints jostle one another around the cataract, and each new addition seems to have lessened the impact of the thing everyone has come to see in the first place. You arrive at your vantage point, step out of car or bus, and in many cases get your first view of the falls through the eyepiece of a camera – nature reduced to 35mm of colour film. So the people come and stare, and seem quite lost, unsure of how they should respond, not certain what is expected of them. Once you have stood there and said wow, and lined up the kids for the photo, what are you supposed to do? The setting has diminished the whole thing to the extent that the great rush of water is now just a backdrop, a disappointment that will be relieved only when you get the film developed and show the pictures to the neighbours. By then the falls have acquired a glamour that you never felt in their presence. My somewhat dour Yorkshire companion at the falls remarked, somewhat unkindly – but I know what he meant: 'I've seen better lavatory flushes.' This is perhaps a somewhat long-winded way of saying that those who want to feel the mysteries of the ancient lands as a genuine emotion, which will remain in the mind even without the benefit of the family snapshot album, must prepare for the experience. It will not be handed to you – you must work for it.

Of all the ancient monuments in Britain, quite the most famous is Stonehenge on Salisbury Plain. It has all the elements of high romance. Its origins are mysterious, its methods of construction obscure, its purpose unknown. Everyone, it seems, has a theory on what it was built for – from a homing beacon for flying saucers to a temple for human sacrifice. Modern Druids meet there, though if anything is certain it is that Druids had nothing to do with its construction. Visitors throng to it, and few remain quite unmoved by its strangeness. It is a spot where a little knowledge adds to rather than subtracts from the sense of mystery, for each new fact seems only to compound the problem. It is an amazingly complex site, begun 4,500 years ago as a vast circular ditch and mound. This remained for about two hundred years before the first ring of stones was assembled inside the ditch. There were at least eighty of them, each weighing around 4 tons, and they were brought all the way from the Prescelly Mountains in South Wales, possibly by sea and river, though no one can now say with certainty. An avenue of stones was also built, leading into the ring. Things were not left at that. The old ring was later dismantled, and huge sarsen stones brought from the Marlborough Downs and set up in the formation we see today. In the final stage some of the blue stones were also incorporated into the grand design. This was completed around 1800 BC, and we have no more idea of why the ring was changed than we do of why the first ditch was dug some eight centuries earlier.

Over the years many writers have expressed the sense of awe and wonder they have felt at the great monument. I wish I could join them. I see it, intellectually, as something quite extraordinary, one of the wonders of the world. I see it, but am quite unable to feel it. The atmosphere, the surroundings interfere too much. The site is trapped in a V formed by two busy roads. It has, quite rightly, been given official protection, but officialdom and a sense of deep mystery seldom sit very easily together. Perhaps it is simply that too many people have said too much: all those shrill voices demanding that we accept their ideas of other-worldliness and dark forces have somehow diminished the reality of the place. God knows it is impressive, mightily impressive, and wonderfully mysterious, so why load it up with half-baked, unproven and unprovable theories. I should like to be left alone for a day at Stonehenge but that, alas, can never be now. There are too many distractions. But there is the consolation that if this greatest and most mysterious of our monuments now comes to us slightly shop-soiled, there are other places not very far away, where I can feel the genuine sense of awe. Others no doubt will respond in quite different ways, but as this is such a subjective area, let me just record one place and one day. It was a day on which the word 'wilderness' really did seem as if it might be able to comprehend something more than rock, heather, wind and sun.

It was a bright July morning when I set out for a solitary walk across Marlborough Downs. Of itself, it could scarcely qualify as a wilderness area, for a road runs across the middle of it, and it is criss-crossed by bridleways. Much of it is farmed, and even at its highest point it fails to reach the 1,000-ft mark. Yet there is a special atmosphere here, enhanced by the knowledge that it is an isolated patch of wild country, a rough island in a fertile sea. It was not, in any case, ever my intention to make a great deal of the walk itself. I regarded it principally as a kind of prelude to the main theme, an introduction to put me in the right frame of mind for what was to come. It somehow seemed appropriate that one should approach the ancient monuments on foot, savouring the thought of them and trying

to sense something of their place and importance in the land. The walk itself was intended to be a gentle, undemanding upland stroll. That, at any rate, was the theory.

    I had another good reason for keeping the walking part of the day to reasonable proportions. I knew that much of the area bore the marks of early settlements and I wanted time to explore, to look around without the nagging necessity of having to hurry on towards some final destination. I wanted to spend some time on Fyfield Down, before making the final approach to Avebury and its surrounding antiquities. The lower slopes of the downs offer their own temptations to linger, though here at first it was simply the attractions of a quiet, gently heaving agricultural landscape. Wheat and barley were being tossed by a strong wind, which turned and bent the stalks so that dark green waves were sent scudding across the pale green fields. The worn pathway showed the brilliant bright gleam of chalk, and hard flint was caught in sharp reflection in the morning sun. And on all sides there was a pathetic sheep chorus. The lambs had only recently been separated from their mothers, and they kept up a continuous lament as they stared at each other through the wire fence. Flocks of lapwings settled, bobbing busily at a field until, for no apparent reason, they all

The western edge of Marlborough Downs.

rose in one great flock, circled briefly and then settled down again to their hunt for titbits.

Although this is very much a landscape where man makes his mark through gates and fences and ordered fields, it still seems an unhurried, remote part of England. It comes in part from the extraordinary width of the views in the clear air. The land rolls away in ever receding and ever paler horizons, until the field patchwork becomes an indistinguishable blur and the farthest hills then look as if they might indeed be wild. And as you climb the gentle slope the sense of loneliness increases. I paused and listened to the birdsong cut through the low moan of the wind, and heard also the distant rattle of a tractor. I looked, and there it was a mile or more away, yet far from diminishing that sense of loneliness the sight seemed to reinforce it; man and machine seemed so isolated among those wide horizons.

Fyfield Down is quite definitely a place to stop, sit and take stock of your surroundings, then to wander around. It is no great place to be if you are in a hurry, simply because its significance is not immediately apparent – a bare hill, spattered with rocks, as if a giant had once emptied out a bagful on his way across the downs. The open character of the hill is broken just below the summit by thickset woodland. There is no immediate call to the senses, demanding that you stop to take in the wonders of the scene, but there is a call to the imagination, for this is the perfect introduction to the ancient world that lies up ahead. Local names are an enticement, names such as Grey Wethers, which sounds as if it might have been invented by Tolkien. It means no more than grey sheep, and very apt the name is too, for the grey boulders left behind by erosion do seem, at a distance, all but indistinguishable from the head-down, munching sheep that litter the slope along with the rocks. But not all the rocks you see owe their position or their shape to the natural actions of wind and weather. It was here the sarsen stones of Stonehenge were quarried, and there are still remains of great stones, excavated but abandoned. Looking at these stones and then turning away to stare across the Downs one is forced to speculate to some extent on what compelled men to make this enormous effort. To move stones at all without the benefit of block and tackle, let alone more complex machinery, seems a daunting enough task. But when you consider that they were not merely to be edged into a new position close at hand, but were to be taken some twenty miles across the hills, and that in the days before there was any wheeled transport, the operation seems almost incredible. As I stood on the top of the hill among the stones and thought about that task, I was no nearer to an understanding of their motives, but I did feel an immense respect for these ancient people. I am no archaeologist, but I

Stonehenge.   know something of engineering. I could see that they must have

commanded some skill, but they must also have commanded a huge store of determination. Given the resources that they had available, I would not think much of my chances of organizing a gang to move those massive blocks. I felt again a sense of wonder at the motives that impelled men to make such an effort.

This area, too, has evidence of another aspect of the life of prehistory, for people settled here and farmed the upland. The marks of their fields, delineated by ridge and ditch, can still be seen, though to the inexpert the signs are not always easy to interpret. The land has so many stories to tell us if only we can read the languages in which the tales are written. Some can read the story of the wildlife of the area from the marks left on the ground, others can understand the way of life of previous generations from the slightest physical evidence. Most of us struggle on a long way in the rear, picking up the crumbs of information dropped by the experts marching on ahead. But, at least, if we are prepared to spend time on observation, we can move towards some understanding of the land, however slight it may be. There are those who are never worried by such considerations, but simply accept the physical presence of the land as a challenge to their own resources, something to be overcome for the pure pleasure of hard, physical exercise. Man may have left his mark on the land over the ages, but that is a misfortune to be endured, an interruption to the essential wild nature of the place. I felt much the same when I first began walking, but more and more I find myself fascinated by the problem of reading and understanding the landscape as a sort of ever-changing history book. I think my enjoyment of a morning spent on Fyfield Down would be considerably lessened if it were nothing more than a rock-strewn hill surrounded by fields.

However intriguing such explorations might be, sometimes it is as well to bring them to a close. I became aware of a change in the light. The sun still shone but as I looked across to the east, I found that the sky had taken on a strange, yellowish cast. The receding hills were now tinged with delicate, subtle colours as if they had been specially ordered to pose for one of those ladylike watercolours much beloved of Jane Austen's heroines. If the view to the east was out of Jane Austen, that to the west had come straight from a Gothic novel. A vast tower of cloud was piling up, the top flayed out and flattened to the distinctive anvil shape of the thunder cloud, *cumulonimbus*. Already it was turning the day to an ominous indigo and there was little room for doubt over what was to come, for the darkness was being driven steadily onwards by the wind. It seemed a good time to start making tracks towards Avebury, 3 miles distant at the foot of the hill.

I had hardly started on my way before the storm broke with breathtaking ferocity. Thunder roared and the view was obliterated in the rain. The sheep lined up with military precision in straight lines, woolly soldiers turning their backs to the weather. A few attempted a little desultory cropping, but the majority just stood, their jaws steadily working, bored spectators in a damp world. The white chalk of the path that had gleamed so brightly just an hour ago was now a greasy, grey slither. Water teemed in rivulets underfoot and the horizontal rain found out every gap in my clothing to trickle in and wet me. Part way down my path crossed that of the Ridgeway along which a second dripping walker appeared, peering out through rain-blurred spectacles. We exchanged the usual cheerful phrases, and I wondered if his hearty good humour was as spurious as my own. Only his dogs, two bedraggled labradors, seemed totally unaffected by the weather, sniffing out rabbits and hares and darting off after a likely scent. Their enthusiasm seemed undiminished either by rain or their total inability to get anywhere near their prey. We parted and I trudged and slid on down the hill towards a bright light that shone through the dark as welcoming as the harbour lights seen by a sailor out on a stormy sea. The light was nothing more dramatic than the pub at Avebury, but it was a wonderfully welcome thought. It is astonishing how quickly one can become cold and miserable on a July morning in England, even when one is no more than a couple of miles from the promise of comfort. Today we have a rudimentary understanding of the forces that shape our climate and weather, but thousands of years ago when the great circle of Avebury was being built, such powers must have seemed part of some immense mystery. We can only speculate about the beliefs of such people, guess at the sophistication of their thinking, but up there on the downs in the centre of the storm I could myself almost come to believe in foul weather as a malignant being, a dark force turned loose upon me. I had in front of me the prospect of a roof over my head, a pint in my hand and hot food in my stomach, and all in exchange for a few pieces of paper stuck into my back pocket. Without such comforting thoughts, how would I cope with the natural world? I had hoped that my stroll over the downs would put me in a receptive frame of mind, help me to a glimmering of comprehension of the mystery of the place. I had certainly not planned such an assault and battery by the elements, but it was undoubtedly proving effective. I have no more true knowledge about Avebury than I had before I started the walk, but I felt much more of a sympathetic understanding for a people who felt the need to rearrange nature, to come to terms with natural forces. A true stalwart would have gone on in the wet gloom, making the most of this unexpected sharpening of the sensibilities to soak up the atmosphere of the ancient stones. I went into the pub and soaked up a pint of bitter instead.

The great bank and standing stones of Avebury.

When I came out the storm was over, the sun had returned and the strange, almost magical atmosphere had dissipated. But something odd still lingered round Avebury in the clarity of the newly-washed air. It is not easy to come to terms with Avebury in the way that it is with, say, Stonehenge. There the stones form a coherent, isolated group, their impressiveness very much on display. At Avebury the sheer size of the ancient monument tells against it, for it can be taken in only a little at a time by exploration. In all the site covers more than 28 acres, enclosed by a circular bank and ditch of almost a mile in perimeter. Once you could have viewed the whole thing with ease, but now the modern village occupies much of the centre – modern that is in relation to the ancient works. There is one prominent building that stands just outside the circle – the Saxon church. This would seem to be part of a pattern established by Pope Gregory when he gave his advice to the early Christians of Britain not to destroy pagan temples. Idols, he said, should be destroyed, but the temples themselves should be consecrated and turned from heathen to Christian places of worship. He felt that there was more chance of making converts of the local inhabitants if they were encouraged to continue visiting the old places of pagan worship, simply substituting a new god for the old. They could then be expected to move on to the new church itself, established alongside the old. The pragmatism lasted a long while, but not for ever. How ironical it is that in the sixth and seventh centuries, when a large proportion of the population still practised what we call heathen or pagan religions, the stones should have been treated with sensible tolerance. A thousand years later when no one any longer had the least notion of the significance of the stones and no one practised the old religions, zealots set about destroying them with great enthusiasm. Today, thanks to their efforts, Avebury has lost some of its grandeur, but even the most fervent iconoclasts were quite unable totally to destroy its magnificence.

What were they destroying? A pagan temple they thought. But is it? Or is it, as has been suggested at Stonehenge, a sort of giant, astronomical calculator? I have no idea, and inspection can now tell you only what is there, not why it is there. So what we are left with is a vast, circular earth bank with a deep ditch inside, pierced by entrances at the four cardinal points of the compass. Within is the Great Circle of sarsen stones, quite unlike those at Stonehenge. Here they have not been shaped and dressed, but selected as appropriate for their function and set into the ground as uprights. This circle is 1,400 feet across, and inside are two smaller circles, each 35 feet in diameter. The precise arrangement of the pattern of stones is uncertain, for the wholesale destruction of the sixteenth and seventeenth centuries multiplied the riddles of this puzzling site. So many stones, weighing up to 40 tons apiece, were quarried, lugged laboriously down the hill, set in place, and then centuries later pulled down again. The pattern in which they were set was clearly most carefully defined, and the actual setting showed a great deal of skill. Such a degree of skill was not always shown by those whose only object was the destruction of the circle. One of the demolition squad managed to topple one of the huge stones, but was not sufficiently agile to get out of its way. He was squashed flat. Yet even the knowledge that the builders of Avebury were more competent than its destroyers tells us little about the actual time of construction. Modern calculations suggest that something like one and a half million man-hours of work went into the building. That is a great deal of work – and suggests the presence of a great many workers. It has been further suggested that thousands were involved, but such vast numbers were not essential to do the actual work. A hundred men working every day could have completed the task in five years. But there would need to have been others involved in feeding, clothing, and caring for these labourers in stone. The numbers begin to multiply until the notion of several hundreds at work, some in the actual construction, others providing the necessities of life, seems quite reasonable. And the extraordinary thing is that no trace of their presence is to be found – no homesteads, no everyday traces of life in the form of potsherds or middens, nothing. There are simply the stones themselves. It is as if, having completed their great work, the builders faded away, leaving the purity of the mystery unsullied by even the memory of the commonplaces of human existence. Perhaps the site was always deemed too important, too holy for mere mortals to live even close at hand, so that the workers were forced to walk each day from more distant homes. If that was so, those in charge of the works had a command of logistics that would be the envy of any modern contractor. But that is speculation, and in the absence of evidence we must be content to take the site as we find it.

Avebury on its own is so striking a place that very little effort is required to conjure up at least a generalized picture of how it must have been 4,000 years ago. You can envisage it, set in virgin country, the mightiest structure for miles around. You can see it, get an inkling of its significance, set in the smooth valley beneath the rough hill, and imagine it as a monument intended to propitiate the violent forces of nature. But you can never be sure that you have ever penetrated to the truth of the mystery. You can just begin to appreciate that this site represents man's Herculean efforts to come to terms with the wilderness and the mysteries that surround him, but no sooner has that idea gained a hold than you discover that it does not, in fact, exist on its own, but is a part of an even grander design.

From the southern entrance at Avebury an avenue of stones leads away to West Kennet. Many people would say that this is the best way to approach Avebury, led down through the lines of standing stones – that this is, in fact, the way in which it was meant to be approached. Possibly so, though I would always contend that if you want to think yourself back into an understanding of what the site might have meant to those who were alive when it was first built, you must approach it

Silbury Hill.

through the wilderness that was home to the builders of the henge. In any case, this was more than an approach road to Avebury, it was a link road joining Avebury to a second circle known as The Sanctuary. Alas, the traces of the second circle have all but gone, and there is a hideous feeling of anti-climax in striding up The Avenue to meet nothing more romantic than a transport caff! Better then to turn off The Avenue, now more prosaically known as the B4003, used by the cars and coaches of the visitors, and stride across Waden Hill or follow the river valley to a monument as remarkable in its way as Avebury – Silbury Hill.

One can visit Avebury, and at least one can see some sort of relationship between it and other henges and stone circles. But Silbury is unique. It is a conical hill, 130 feet high and covering some 5 acres, and it was built entirely by human effort, probably around 2500 BC. It is the largest man-made mound in Europe and its significance, as with so many of these ancient monuments, remains unknown. Early theories all suggested that it was a burial chamber, but numerous excavations, which have left it as full of holes as a Gruyère cheese, have disclosed no evidence to support that view. The most recent excavations of 1968–70, carried out with full television coverage, added evidence on several points, but provided no clue to the greatest mystery of all. Why was it built? Its shape is very like that of the popular representation of a flying saucer, a fact which has not gone unremarked by the UFO watchers who have been remarkably keen to publicize their theories. Those of us who cannot see why a civilization sufficiently advanced to travel through space should wish to commemorate their visit with a huge earthwork remain unconvinced. So the mysteries are multiplied, and it is something of a relief to walk a little further to find another famous antiquity on view, but one which at least had a known function, West Kennet long barrow.

The barrow is a Neolithic tomb, and careful excavation has revealed that it was in use as a burial place for many centuries. It takes the form of a long mound covering the burial chamber, the entrance to which was originally closed by sarsen stones. From here one can gain a physical perspective on the sites of the region, for you can look straight across to Silbury Hill, Avebury and the swell of the downs beyond. The barrow itself is accessible, close to a main road, so that, as so often happens, its sense of atmosphere might have been lost. It is up to the individual to decide whether or not that has happened in this case, but it was not the case for me. Perhaps I was fortunate in that the sequence of events of the day had put me in a receptive frame of mind – though I had certainly not planned to include a thorough soaking in my itinerary. Yet that seems, in retrospect, to have been important. By the time I reached West Kennet I was still gently steaming as the last of the rain evaporated, so that the memory of the chill and sting of the rain was still with me. I would soon return to a hot meal and dry clothes, but the discomfort emphasized that even this gentle land could know other moods. And, in times past, it would not have been so gentle, nor would comforts have been so readily available to its few inhabitants. Even the necessities of life were hard won from this far from friendly land. And if the world refused to yield to man with ease, what was he expected to do to make it more tractable? The forces against which he had to tussle were as vast as the dark clouds that had massed over the downs earlier in the day. No small, insignificant gesture could propitiate such a power, and it is very tempting to think of the sarsens, the stone rings, the ditches and embankments as part of man's response to a dimly-understood natural world. The true wilderness has long since gone, but those who come here can still re-create it in their minds.

Marlborough Downs can be enjoyed as a setting for a summer's day outing, a pleasant walk beneath big skies. But, as I discovered on that day in July, even the most apparently innocuous landscape can transform itself into a true wilderness in an amazingly short space of time. This alone would make it an interesting area for walking, but it is that extra element that turns it into something unique. It is that sense that although modern man no longer feels it necessary to propitiate the harsher elements in nature, there was a time when man's hold on the land was so precarious that the most monumental efforts were needed to propitiate the gods who would allow him this brief resting-place on the planet's surface. It is here, if anywhere, that you become aware of the essential insignificance of man in the universe at large. So it is that you can stand on a piece of well-mown grass, within earshot of roads and traffic, and feel more alone than you will ever feel on the most remote mountain peak. And that surely qualifies this land of ancient monuments for inclusion within any reasonable definition of wilderness.

5. Mid Wales

Mid Wales might reasonably be described as the Great Unknown. South Wales: that's easy: it's miners and male voice choirs and the Arms Park on Saturday. North Wales is mountains and slate. Then there are odd bits left over, like Pembroke, which can be dismissed as a piece of England accidentally tacked on to Wales as an afterthought. So runs popular mythology, and the bit in the middle seems always to get left out. It is an area rather reminiscent of those ancient maps where the blanks were filled with the vague, but chilling, pronouncement – here be dragons. If there are dragons here, then they are assuredly Welsh ones, for this is a part of the country which has retained more of its individuality and character than any other part of the land. It is an area which I have dipped into rather than explored in detail, but one which never fails to fascinate – and one where, it seems, one really can find a sense of solitude.

My first acquaintance with the region was a visit to a friend's cottage in the hills between Llanfair Caereinion and Caersws – and before I incur the wrath of the nationalists may I say that the owners were of impeccable Welsh descent. I should perhaps add, however, that if they had not taken it over, it would have been left to crumble into ruins, for even now it lacks a great many amenities. Running water is a tap at the end of a pipe which leads down the hillside from a spring, and to describe the sanitary arrangements as primitive is to show a degree of kindness. The situation is remote, with just a farm some distance away and a still active quarry somewhat nearer at hand. Before coming there I had almost forgotten what it was to live in such a superbly remote area, where the chances of meeting anyone at all other than the occasional shepherd or farmer were decidedly slim. The whole place has this atmosphere which I can only describe as an air of consistency. Nothing went on there that was not directly related to the land: you farmed it, dug rock out of it, or simply walked it for pleasure. True, the farmer had a Land-Rover, rocks were taken from the quarry by truck, and we used to drive by car down into the nearest village to do our shopping, but these were incidentals, small distractions in a stable pattern that seemed to stretch back over the centuries.

To describe the area as unchanged is, of course, misleading. This small area may not have changed much, but you have no need to travel very far to see such changes as there have been. To the south the road is busy with container trucks, plying to and fro between the Laura Ashley factory and the cities of Britain. At Llanfair the old railway which had once taken pigs and their owners to market has now become one of the Great Little Trains of Wales, and the tourists travel behind the slow chuffing of the old steam locomotives in carriages which once did duty on the mountain railways of central Europe. There is, however, no need to dwell on these new exemplars of the

The head of the Pennant valley.

changes that have come, or the changes that will come, to this region. One cannot say with any certainty where the future prosperity of the area will lie, whether with the backward, nostalgic glance of the steam railway or with the modern textile factory, but it does seem that the other, wild Wales is with us for a good while yet. And this, I take it, is what a lot of people want – the nationalists eager to preserve language, traditions and the essential character of land and people, as well as the 'foreigners' from across the Marches, hunting for peace and quiet. Yet there are nagging doubts that both sides are, in their very different ways, trying to preserve a way of life that is over and done, even entirely mythical. Was the past ever really all that pure, all that enticing? Didn't the seemingly virgin land ever do a little whoring on the side? When I came back to Mid Wales in the autumn of 1982 I came with expectations of finding a part of Britain where I would be free to wander where I wished, an unspoilt wilderness. I was looking for a spot where I could choose my own routes with no help from the writers of guidebooks. To an extent, I had my wish. But I also found a country far more complex than I had ever imagined.

I had mentioned the idea of a long week-end in Mid Wales to an old friend, Peter, who was immediately enthusiastic, for he had spent a little time in the region and was very keen to see more. I had no very definite plans beyond a vague notion of getting up into the hills and as far away from the rest of the world as possible. Peter, on the other hand, had at least one very positive notion of exactly where he wanted to go. He had some while back been to camp with his children in the

Llyn Clywedog, the reservoir to the south of the Pennant valley.

Pennant valley, and all the time he had been there he had wanted to explore the upper valley but had never quite got round to doing so. Here, it seemed, was the ideal opportunity, and as it lay very much within the area I had in mind and as I certainly had no better suggestion to put forward, the Pennant valley was marked down as our first destination.

Our chosen weekend was the first in October, a magical time of year when the freshness of summer is still lingering but there is a keenness and bite to the air, a clarity that shows off the first brilliance of the autumnal tints. Browning dreamed of April, but I would take early autumn any time. And we were to be blessed with the best of it. The sun shone from a cloud-scudded sky, the wind blew with an exhilarating touch that a month later would have been an uncomfortable chill – it was a combination that promised well for the day. And the day itself held out a promise of something a little extra. For we were not, to be honest, altogether certain where our chosen path would lead us. Peter had stayed in the broad, lower valley, and had seen two fine waterfalls further up the river: it would be possible, he thought, to scramble up beside the two falls to reach the valley head. The upper part of this valley was shown on the map as very narrow with cliffs down one side and a very steep slope on the other, but there appeared to be an accessible route if we kept very close to the line of the river. Once at the top we would follow the watercourse as it bent

A view that demonstrates that a reservoir need not be ugly.

round towards the hamlet of Dylife, then cross the high plateau by a small lake before heading off towards a long ridge that would lead back through woodland to Pennant itself in the bottom of the valley. Such at any rate was the theory. Practice was not to match the agreed plan.

The start was certainly perfect as we parked the car and set off along the country lane that followed the course of the river. The fields caught in the early morning sunlight were a wonderfully lush green, with a richness that I had seen previously only in Ireland. The sun streamed across the low hills to the east to pick out the grazing sheep to form an abstract pattern of white polka dots on an emerald cloth. One tends to overlook sheep in the British uplands, simply because they are such a common feature of the scene. They are also, however, a vital part of the hill farmer's economy, but sheep are troublesome creatures that require much tending. While staying some years earlier at a farm further south in the Brecon Beacons, I was intrigued to find that the farmer still relied on the hardy Welsh pony to reach his scattered flock. There are other reminders, not so far away, of the even greater importance that sheep once had in the whole life of the region. The area still has a number of small woollen mills, but most are as much dependent on the tourists that come to see the old machinery at work as they are on the cloth that they sell. One exception to the general rule that the textile industry of Wales is on its knees is the new, busy and profitable Laura Ashley factory. Some have complained that it introduces a foreign element into the area, but it seems to me to be merely a continuation of a long tradition. For the moment, however, the sheep seemed less important as a symbol of a changing economy than as an attractive feature of a lovely scene. Only the most callous could look the placid beasts in the eye and let their minds linger on the uniquely sweet flavour of fresh Welsh lamb.

The lane soon petered out into a track that ran past old farm buildings and a semi-ruined limekiln, built into the slope of the hill. Someone had been at work restoring the old house and very comfortable it looked too. From the outside there was no means of telling whether the restorers were local or English, whether it was to be a family home or a weekend cottage. I find it sad to think that in one set of circumstances it will be looked on as a welcome development, in another as a candidate for burning. For the house is there now, it exists: a decent, solid building, and whoever the present occupants are and whatever use they put it to, they will go in time and the fine old building will be used by others. I regard these vernacular buildings as an important part of the local heritage. If preserved there is a very good chance that they would find 'acceptable' use by 'acceptable' people: once destroyed, a piece of the valley's past has gone. I know all the arguments about outsiders and weekenders, who

The steep scree slopes up which the author scrambled – with difficulty.

take from the area but put nothing back – English villages have suffered quite as much as Welsh. There too the holiday cottage has done its bit to upset the old order, so that the labourer's home has now become a desirable *bijou* residence and the labourer is often forced out of the village altogether. Yet nothing will persuade me that burning down the old cottage can ever be the answer.

I jotted down these thoughts in the form of a few notes as we walked down the lane, but it was no more than a brief shadow on the morning, for there were soon other considerations to keep the mind busy. The track was heading away from the river, so we turned down towards the water and the rich meadows. It was easy to see why Peter had never got very far on his previous visit, for it was an idyllic spot. Meadows led down to the tree-fringed river, and the early morning sun was already bringing a pleasant warmth to the sheltered valley. The air stirred gently beneath the protecting hills. We found a crossing-point, where boulders staggered through the water in an accidental arrangement that turned them into perfect stepping-stones, and we sauntered along the bank on the comfortable turf. Away to the west a track could clearly be seen, wandering up the bluff shoulder of the hill, very much in the direction of our first destination, but we were not to be deterred by such promises of ease and stuck to our riverside track.

The track we were following was, at best, a vague indication rather than a definite way forward. Soon the valley sides began to close in, and the only tracks to be seen now were the narrow lines of sheep paths. The slope above was becoming steeper and the easy ground beside the stream steadily more constricted. The valley itself was tilting upwards, so that the river was now gurgling and splashing over the rocks with fine abandon. The prospects for forward progress were beginning to look decidedly dim. The high steep banks enclosed us, and they rose some thirty feet or so above the water, cutting off any view beyond. We reached a point where even the sheep seemed to have given up. I tried to edge along by the water to what looked like better ground up ahead, but the shaley bank began to crumble beneath feet and hands, so I edged back to avoid a ducking. Inevitably the going on the opposite bank looked quite good – when does it not? The problem was how to get over there without an ignominious and time-consuming retreat. There was only one answer, paddle, so paddle we did with icy water swirling round our shins as we gingerly stepped from one slippery, submerged rock to the next. Safely across, I promptly contrived to drop one boot, which set off like a canoe on a slalom and I only just managed to grab it in time. The little incident proved if nothing else that the time spent on waterproofing the boots had not been wasted.

If the other side of the river inevitably looks better than the side you are on, it soon enough appears with equal inevitability that this is an illusion. This occasion was to prove no exception, as the gorge narrowed ever more severely, and we were forced to admit that there was no way we could advance in that particular direction. Again the solution appeared straightforward. From the bottom of our cleft we could see the rim, which would presumably offer an alternative route along the valley but at a somewhat higher level. The bank was steep with a layer of unstable shale, but by zig-zagging to reduce the angle progress proved comparatively simple, even if it was frequently a case of two steps up and one slide back. Reaching that rim proved, however, only to be the start of the next problem, not the solution we had expected.

It was not, as it had appeared, the top of a bank at all, merely the spot where the angle of the slope changed. Once there, our little valley suddenly took on an amazingly menacing look now that it could be seen to its full height for the first time. The hillside opposite swept upwards from the river for a full 600 feet in what looked like a smooth, pathless wall. Being able to see the whole of that darkly gleaming scree slope made what we could see of our side look equally daunting. It was unpromising but not, we felt, impossible, and to our delight we found that the local farmer had set a fence all down the edge of the scree to keep his sheep away from danger. It was not a job I would have fancied tackling, but I was very glad that someone else had. Now we could head straight up by heaving ourselves along from post to post, a tiring business but considerably less wearing and less nerve-racking than the slide and slither of the steep slope of loose shale. We kept this up until the slope eased and we were able to head off at a more comfortable angle, moving diagonally across towards the tree line. The cool breeze was more than welcome for we were both, by this time, pretty well drenched in sweat and displaying all too many signs that we were not quite as fit as we had supposed. Pausing for breath, we looked out to where a buzzard mocked our panting progress, as it rose with a scarcely discernible flap of its wings to ride the thermals up the hillside. To the south we could now see our original objective, the waterfalls that fell dramatically in the narrow gorge. Seen from this viewpoint, it now seemed just as well that our plans had been frustrated as soon as they were. It was clear that the river was tightly enclosed between rock walls, and our experience had already shown that the rock was rotten and crumbling. Nevertheless, although we had failed in our original plan, our efforts were more than rewarded at that moment, standing above the steep, smooth slope, by the sheer magnificence of the hill scenery. Some of the pleasure was slightly dampened by the thought that we could have come by car and walked a short way to reach this same point. That seemed all wrong; everyone should have to work as hard as we had done to earn such a reward. But at least we had the consolation of knowing that we had well and truly earned the right to sit and take things easy, enjoying the panorama.

We did not sit for long, for there was also a certain matter of thirsts to be attended to, so we moved off over the seemingly easy-going path until we reached the wall that marked the edge of the level land of the plateau. We hopped over the wall into a field of cows – well, mainly cows, for there was also one representative, and a very large one, of the opposite sex. It is an often repeated theory that you will never have any trouble from a bull if there are cows in the field. You simply ignore the beast and walk steadily and firmly on your way. This we did, and all seemed well until I looked over my shoulder to find the bull trotting along in our wake, snorting to itself. Some 50 yards ahead was the edge of the field and a five-barred gate. I have no idea what the world record is for the 50-yard dash and high hurdle, but I believe I could have claimed it.

Saddle Tor, on Dartmoor.

The Cumbrian mountains from Langdale

The Dee Valley, near Llangollen, North Wales.

Moel Ddu from the south, the Snowdon range seen in the background.

The Conwy Valley, North Wales.

A viaduct near Blaenau Ffestiniog.

Ben Nevis from Achriabhach.

The Peak District, Snake Pass.

Snowdon, seen across Llynnau Mymbyr.

View of Ranworth Broad from the top of Ranworth Church.

A view of Cape Wrath across the Kyle of Durness.

The River Dart, near Bellever.

The River Irt, running into Wastwater.

Soon we were at the end of the deep valley, as the river turned at a right angle, and we followed it and the road which now appeared alongside towards Dylife, a melancholy home of memories. It was a place that had been called into existence for just one commodity – lead. The Romans came here, and the faint traces of their fortlet can be seen on top of a knoll to the south of the village. But mostly what you can see are the remains of the lead mines worked in the middle of the nineteenth century, briefly revived in the 1930s and now abandoned again. The legacy of the years of work can be seen in the mountains of spoil – and in the river which looked so beautiful and pure when seen in the valley 800 feet below. Now its true nature was revealed. It is a dead river, poisoned by the lead from the mines. And all around the land seemed dead, not just from lead pollution but from the knowledge that, with the closure, the community had died too. It seemed all but impossible to imagine that the place had ever been alive. There were three hundred men employed here half a century ago. There were houses, a church and, being Wales, three chapels. Now there are the graveyards – the industrial graveyard spread out all around and the one where the people are buried. But the pub remains, and it was there that we discovered that though the mining community had gone, it is not forgotten.

There were only a few of us in there, ourselves and half a dozen locals, including the old men who carried the memories and told the stories. This had never been a true community, it appeared, for few had ever settled here. The men had left their families behind in the surrounding district to come up to work, returning when they could for visits. It was hard work and a rough life and, not surprisingly, a few miners looked for consolation among the local girls. One, it appears, found the consoler more appealing than the family he had left behind. The wife, hearing no word from Dylife, came up to investigate for herself. Here she was murdered, and her body thrown down the shaft of one of the abandoned workings. Whether the evidence of the husband's guilt would have satisfied a court of law will never be known – for the miners applied their own justice. The man was hanged. And did this tale which seemed to belong to Dodge City or the Californian goldrush really take place in Wales in the twentieth century? The old men could not swear as to exactly when it happened, but were quite positive that it had happened just as they said. Other stories of the village in the days when it was still alive and thriving could be vouched for with more certainty. The zigzag path, the easy route from Pennant, was the postman's path, which the local postman would walk every day with the mail. So the stories rolled on, memories of the place that had lived briefly and then died. Rather than diminish the sense that we had reached a lonely spot in the middle of

Wales, the knowledge that it had once been busy and yet had left so few traces behind served only to increase the sense of its present remoteness.

Suitably refreshed, we decided to keep to our original plan for the return, in the hope and expectation that it would turn out to be rather more successful than our morning plan. From the pub we set out northwards across the plateau moorland where the wind that had never troubled us in the deep gully now blew with something like gale force. The plateau itself was rounded off at the edges where it dropped down to meet a ragged, rocky escarpment. Sheep picked their way delicately through the sliding scree, not always it seemed with complete success, as a corpse at the foot of one of the crags proved. The edge was then sliced open by a tributary stream that tumbled down a narrow gully to the distant river. We scrambled down, crossed the stream, and paused in the shelter for a cup of tea from the thermos. We sat at peace with the world, enjoying the respite from the wind and the cheerful splash and gurgle of the hill stream. It was beautifully quiet and we seemed quite alone in the world, until I looked up to find I was being scrutinized by a bright-eyed buzzard. The big bird perched on a rock on the opposite side of the stream, seemingly quite unperturbed by our presence. We eyed each other, and the buzzard became bored with the game long before I did. He spread his wings and with what seemed no more than a couple of beats, he was away and soaring, crabbing across the sky aslant the wind. Earthbound we plodded on, climbing out of the gulley. This was the typical moorland now of wiry grass tufts, alternating with brighter-coloured marshland. At the top of the moor was the source of our stream, Llyn Nant-ddeilliog, and from here all around was just a splendid vista of moor and distant hills. Perhaps it had none of the true drama of the more mountainous peaks to the north, but the sense of isolation, of standing in wild surroundings in land unmarked by track or path, makes this part of the country unique.

Clouds sailed high on the wind as we found our ridge and set off down its rocky spine towards the valley. On the ridge we were exposed to the full force of the wind, and felt that at any time we might be joining the clouds for a sail across the valley. But we arrived at the foot of the ridge without mishap and came to the start of the forest that clothed much of the lower slopes. I am not much addicted to forest walks such as this, where narrow paths lead between densely packed conifers. The darkness seemed to creep right up to the very edge of the pathway, and it all appeared dank and gloomy. Perhaps the gloom originates with all those stories of childhood, the Grimm fairy tales and Hansel and Gretel, where nothing good ever seems to be found among the fir trees. Certainly I found little to cheer me as I

The lush meadows of the Pennant valley.

bounced down the steep path. There were no flowers to be seen, only some peculiarly evil-looking fungi, some with bright orange tips, others a repugnant, slimy brown. I was quite prepared to believe there was a gingerbread house in there somewhere and had no wish to find it. I suppose it is largely a matter of habit. I began my walking in the hills of the Pennines. They were my first love, and it is those open moorland scenes that still evoke the deepest response. On the other hand a Swedish friend of mine who came to live in the district, started by loathing the moors and longed for the dark, enclosed forest walks of his homeland. Now he has come to love the Pennines and not only walks but *runs* the Three Peaks, an achievement I have no intention of trying to emulate. So, given time, I might share his enthusiasm for the forest, though I shall never enjoy the sight of the conifer plantations that blanket so many of our hills, their edges ruled in absurd straight lines, slicing up the natural flow of the contours. Anyway, I was glad enough to leave the woods and come out onto the lower pasture.

The wind was down in the valley now, slicking back the grass like brilliantined hair. The rich green and the small farms made an amazing contrast to the sterile land we had recently left above the valley. It is always tempting to come to an area such as this and say, 'Ah, here is the real Wales!' But which was the true Wales – was it the lead mine on the hill or the farm in the valley, or was it the combination of the two? The sensible answer must be that it is a combination of these factors and many, many more that give a nation its identity. No doubt the locals could point to certain features in buildings and landscape that represented some sort of quintessential Welshness, but such a task was beyond me.

I was reminded of the difficulties that outsiders such as myself frequently experience in identifying the national characteristics that separate Wales from the rest of Britain on the following day. After a day's excellent walking I felt free to indulge one of my other enthusiasms, and went off to take a journey on the Talyllyn Railway.

The uplands near Dylife.

And it was here that I felt far more conscious of a different community with a different way of life than I ever had in the Pennant valley. The delights of hill walking have, in their essentials, little or nothing to do with the artificial features and frontiers that men set up to divide the land into distinct regions. The exhilaration of walking over the moor in the wind was exactly what I would have felt on any similar walk anywhere in Britain. Yet the little railway seemed particularly Welsh, serving as it did that most Welsh of industries, slate. The pleasures of that day were at once similar and dissimilar to those of the day spent in and around the Pennant valley. Having taken the narrow-gauge train up the hill from Tywyn we set out for a few hours' walk up through forest paths onto the hills. Yet the railway was always there in our minds, carrying as it does not just passengers but memories of the days when the hills, like the hill above Pennant, were busy with the activities of men. The forest trails follow the track of old tramroads out to the quarries, and here one does somehow sense something quite foreign, a way of life that was unique to such areas. I felt also that there was something about the place that spoke very directly about the past, and I sensed something of the old way of life which had brought men into such intimate connection with the very structure of the hills.

I can sympathize with those who wish to preserve what they see as national characteristics, and it is perhaps presumptious of an outsider to interfere in such matters. But it did seem to me that the character of this place lay only partly in the nature and customs of the people. It resides equally strongly in the land itself, in the existence of the tiny railway linking the life of the valley to the life of the hills. It was as much a part of the true spirit of the place as language or folklore. The Welsh farmhouse down below seems as much a part of the national culture as harpist and bard. Stones can carry the history of a place as effectively as books, and it seems to me to be sheer madness to equate those stones with the identity of their temporary owners. Part at least of the identity of the land lies in the land itself and in this lonely and mercifully undeveloped heart of Wales, the nature of the country imposes itself, ignoring the temporary affairs of men. The lead miners came to dominate the area, but now they have gone and the land is slowly reasserting itself, though it will be a long time yet before the memory of the miners' work disappears from barren land and dead river. But it will fade at last. Ultimately, it is as much by our treatment of the land as by our treatment of the people that the essential nature of the place will be preserved or destroyed.

6. NORTH WALES

I have never been lucky with North Wales. I first came to the area as a schoolboy in the early 1950s. My friends and I had arrived in Bethesda far too late for any public transport, and we were weighed down under heavy packs, since it had seemed only sensible to carry as much free food as we could scrounge from home. Nevertheless, as we were only some five miles from the Nant Ffrancon Pass and Llyn Ogwen, the area where we intended to make our base, we shouldered our loads and marched. We strode off down a main road, bordered by dark, looming hills, distinct against a moonlit sky. It was a strange night. The skies were clear, the weather fine, yet I can still remember the atmosphere of that walk. There was a brooding quality that might have been laid to adolescent fantasies, but it reduced us all to silence. We were close to Llyn Ogwen when we heard the cries for help. They seemed too distinct to be mistaken for a bleating sheep or the cry of a night owl, yet they seemed impossible to locate. No matter how we shouted, the cries seemed always to answer from a different spot. Eventually we decided it must have been some animal, or a practical joker with an odd sense of humour. If there really had been someone in distress out on the hillside, he was showing remarkable mobility. It was only later that we heard about the ghost of a dead climber, supposed to haunt the area. If someone had told me about the ghost in the first place, I would not have been so bothered about the shouts. I have never been greatly convinced by the supernatural, and on the one occasion when I slept in an allegedly haunted house and was subjected to things going bump in the night, it caused me little concern. If there are lingering manifestations of past tragedies, then I really cannot see that they should be much concern to the living. As it was, we were simply delayed in our walk and eventually we had to settle down for a night huddled into the church porch. I decided that if there was anything evil abroad in the air that night, it was not the spirit of a dead climber, but a bad omen. The rain began the next morning, and was to continue for a fortnight of the most miserable weather I can remember.

We had come to the area for rock climbing. In the morning we walked a mile along the river bank to the bridge; in the evening we simply stomped straight through the river, for it was by then impossible to get any wetter. Climbs became grotesque caricatures of their normal selves. Easy, gentle routes such as the Idwal slabs were water chutes, and during that time I learned one very valuable lesson about mountain weather. One day, neither wetter nor drier than the rest, we decided to opt for a simple route – the ascent of Snowdon via the Crib Goch ridge, a route so elementary that it does not even classify as a climb at all, but comes within that broad category so common in Snowdonia of a scramble. This simply means a route which requires you in places to use hands as well as feet to negotiate

Looking across Nant Cynnyd towards the hills of Snowdonia.

obstacles but which, in summer, does not require the special equipment of the climber. We set off blithely enough, but half-way up the ridge the clouds closed in, not perceived by us as clouds but simply as an intensely damp, chilling mist. In a sense it presented no great problem, since the route is easy enough to follow – keep going up the ridge and you will arrive at the top. But we had not made sufficient allowance for the chill factor, the way the damp cold can eat into you and sap your energy. We were young, fit and, so we thought, experienced. In the event we proved fit enough, but we reached the summit shivering and with chattering teeth, and dangerously close to suffering from exposure. We were lucky, and the lesson was learned. That was the last time I treated the British hills with disdain. Since that date I have probably erred on the side of caution, but I come to the hills for pleasure as well as for a challenge – and there is little pleasure to be had when you are lying half-frozen on a hillside praying for rescue.

Snowdon seen across Llynau Mymbyr.

Since that time, thirty years ago, I have returned several times to North Wales, in both summer and winter, but always it seems to the same refrain, 'You should have been here last week. Weather's turned now.' My last excursion was no exception. I set off with high hopes in wonderful weather in early summer, but as we drove down the Llanberis Pass the inevitable change got under way. The scene can best be described in terms of music – we started with Delius and ended with Wagner. Vast clouds, ranging in colour from ominous purple to deepest black rolled up the valley to the accompaniment of the entire celestial percussion section. Scampering out of the car for shelter, I got indoors and found myself peering at the 'view of Snowdon' on which the hotel prided itself. It was no doubt an accurate representation, but I had no means of checking, for the mountain had long since vanished from view. It was no more than I had come to expect.

It is not only unpleasant but can be downright stupid to plan for any major hill walks in such conditions, when visibility on the mountain is reduced to a matter of a few feet. I thought it was ironic that on my last visit to the mountain the weather had been splendid, but I had done no actual walking at all. I had determined to travel all the steam railways of Wales, and had to include the Snowdon Mountain Railway. It offers a most enjoyable rail journey, but I felt consumed with guilt from start to finish. As I was carried upwards, through no efforts of my own, I passed many parties of walkers who waved cheerily at the little train. But I could not help feeling that they were secretly despising such 'effete' means of mountain travel. Nevertheless, it is a fine journey with marvellous views, even if it does end with the hideous anti-climax of the least attractive summit in the British Isles. Perched on top is an ugly grey box of a restaurant, replete with all the glamour and romance of a motorway service station. Musing on such matters, I decided to turn away from Snowdon itself and return to my older stamping-ground of Tryfan and the Glyders. Even if the weather stayed clamped down, I could at least walk round Llyn Idwal and watch the storm brewing up in the Devil's Kitchen.

The area has changed a good deal since I first came here. Traffic on the roads has increased vastly, with the tourist coaches threading the mountain roads, the queues of cars lengthening behind them. There are not just more car-bound tourists, there are more walkers and climbers as well. The area has become thick with specialist shops, selling boots, ropes, anoraks and the assorted hardware which is indispensable to the serious modern climber. When I began climbing, the only ironmongery was the nailed boot, though that was very soon to go out of favour, replaced by the compressed rubber 'Vibram' sole. The hills are far busier now, and the favoured crags ring with the sound of hammer on metal. Climbers of my generation tend to tut-tut over the 'artificiality' of modern techniques. I cannot agree. Rock climbing is an essentially artificial and absurd pastime. The first mountaineers simply wanted to get to the top, but as the vast majority of British summits can be reached by the expenditure of much effort but little skill, it soon became accepted that the object of the exercise should be to find the most difficult route to the summit. So all the time standards were improved, until a point was reached where further progress could be made only through the use of pitons, expansion bolts and the rest. And it was here, among the mountains of North Wales, that some of the great advances were made, led by that fine climber, Joe Brown.

It is difficult for those who have never climbed to understand the fascination of the sport. It is no less difficult for those who have to define it. I can still vividly recall my own first attempts, being taken by a school friend, Tom Morrell, who had already been well and truly bitten by the bug, to try my luck on a local gritstone outcrop. I scrambled up a route on the rocks at Ilkley, loathing every minute of it, petrified at the prospect of falling, not because I would be hurt – I was securely held on a rope from above – but dreading the humiliation. I heaved myself up over the last ledge, sat down, and scarcely knowing why I spoke, asked for more. I never regretted the change from hill walking to climbing. My new sport took me to many of the same places I would have visited as a walker, but now there was that extra element of challenge, seeing how far you could push your body and, more importantly, your will, for much of the success of climbing depends on personal confidence. And there was the *frisson* of danger: and this is the point where the climber and the non-climber often end up in mutual incomprehension.

No climber would ever deny that there is danger in his sport. No one who climbs can fail to be aware of it – or aware of the consequences should something go badly wrong. I have had minor accidents myself, and I can clearly remember the chilling experience of helping to carry two dead bodies down from the crags after a fatal accident in the Cuillin Hills of Skye. But the good climber is the one who takes every precaution to minimize the danger of injury, and with the advance in climbing standards there has also been an advance in safety equipment. The helmet, unknown years ago, is now standard, and the use of artificial aids for safety reasons has greatly increased. Yes, the danger remains, but the climber generally endangers himself, not others. But what about all those poor people who have to turn out as rescue parties? Many will be other climbers who volunteer for the work, and the professional will generally be found climbing for pleasure as well. Those who argue that climbing should be limited in some way, licensed perhaps, in order to protect the rescuers, should take a poll among members of any rescue party. They will find few, if any, supporters.

It is perhaps inevitable that those who have never climbed, and have no wish to do so, should find the philosophy of the climber difficult to understand. On any fine day in Snowdonia you will see them leaning against their cars looking up at the crags of Tryfan, where tiny figures edge their way up the rocks. It has become an accepted part of the scene: rock climbing as a spectator sport. And if you stand among such onlookers you will hear the incomprehension everywhere expressed, tinged with resentment sometimes, as though there was something basically immoral about individuals who choose to separate themselves so far from the crowd. Most of these people are perfectly content simply to drive through the area, stopping in lay-bys to view the scenery and then moving on. They have no wish to make closer contact with the mountains than that. Equally, some hill walkers tend to regard the climbers with less than wholehearted enthusiasm, deriding them as gymnasts who choose to do their exercises in the open air instead of in a sports hall. Sometimes I raise my own voice against some of the more mechanically minded climbers who set out routes which are more like exercises in civil engineering than attempts to come to terms with the natural environment. But then there are also the climbers who regard themselves as an élite among all those who come to the hills, a view I must shamefacedly admit I held in my acned adolescence.

There is a wide divergence of views about the mountains, and sometimes it seems that efforts are being made to construct some sort of merit table. At the bottom are the coach parties and motorists who see the peaks only through moving windows, to be followed at a short distance by those who actually stop and get out of their cars. Up another rung, and we find the hill walkers, who will set out for the peaks, and at the very top are the rock climbers – though they can be sub-divided by shades of excellence from the mere scramblers to those who tackle routes of maximum severity. And all these categories can be found in Snowdonia – and Snowdonia tries to cater for them all. Is such a thing possible, and if it is not possible, where should the priorities lie? Those who construct the table of merit would have no doubt, but their table rests on a fallacy – a fallacy which says that my pleasure is more intense than yours, therefore my demands should have greater weight than yours. But how do we measure degrees of pleasure? That is the great dilemma that still has to be resolved.

It is tempting to suggest that the answer lies in a respect for the place itself, making all else subservient to that. Keep the wilderness, whatever the cost. Had such a policy been followed in the 1890s, then the Snowdon Mountain Railway would never have been built, and the

millions who have enjoyed the trip would have been denied the pleasure. Yet from that same railway you can see the most popular walking route up the railway, which is also a great tourist attraction, so much so, in fact, that erosion has become a serious problem. Which then is doing the greater harm to the mountain, the railway or the walker? A balance must be maintained between the demands of all the groups who come to Snowdonia for pleasure, but a balance where a large weight must be put in the scale-pan for the protection of the land itself. And one more factor seems to be of the greatest importance: whatever decisions are taken, they must be implemented in such a way that there is the minimum interference with the freedom of the individual to find his own way of enjoying and appreciating the mountain scenery.

The easy way up: the Snowdon mountain railway.

Saying that there is no especial merit in any one particular method of enjoying mountain scenery is not at all the same thing as saying that the nature of the enjoyment is the same in all cases, nor that all enjoy it with the same degree of intensity. To the casual visitor, the mountains represent 'a scene', something to be enjoyed in a particular but rather limited way. It is the difference between seeing a handsome man or a beautiful woman pass in the street or knowing them as friends. The walker and the climber can both achieve an intimacy with the hills denied to those who view only from afar. As with all friendships, in time you will see the best and the worst of the individual. And, as in friendships, two people may have a mutual friend whom they regard in quite different ways. The climber may have a deep appreciation of the whole range of mountain scenery, but for much of the time his attention will be concentrated on the small area of rock immediately in front of his face – though a certain preoccupation with the ground below his feet is not unknown. The walker sees rock and water and vegetation as part of a whole complex scene, a scene that constantly alters in the ever-changing light. And there is nowhere where the light changes as often or as dramatically as in the hills of North Wales. To the walker, the climber's concentration can mean that the wide view is often completely lost. Yet the climber's very closeness can bring its own rewards, the minute fingertip exploration of rock faces can help to bring out the enormous differences found between one area and the next. No one who has ever climbed could fail to be aware of the vast differences between the rough gabbro of the Cuillins and the shattered granite of Snowdonia. It is not just texture and basic structure, but the way in which the rock weathers, that affects the climber, the rounded edges of one rock contrasting with the sharp edges of the other. The Welsh mountains offer a most satisfying mixture of types. The hard granite sticks out in sharp outline from the eroded sedimentary rocks, while volcanic action has thrown up giant slabs, seen at their most spectacular on the summit of Glyder Fach. Here they pile up into what has been called the Castle of the Winds, for it seemed to early observers that the slabs and pillars must be the ruins of some ancient temple. To me they seem more like the backbone of one of the scalier dinosaurs, though that is a judgement based on memories. Glyder Fach was lost in cloud when I set out for a walk, and I had no intention of trying for its summit that day. Those who bemoan the foolhardiness of the rock climber often overlook the stupidities of the hill walkers who will not admit that certain conditions make certain routes impossible. Glyder Fach looked singularly out of reach.

I set off from the end of Llyn Ogwen, the mile-long lake that sits beside the busy A5. It is to me one of the great recurring miracles of

A typical Snowdonia scene of shattered rock: Llanberis Pass.

North Wales that, within minutes of leaving the road, you are in the heart of a tract of country as wild as anyone could wish. Little more than half a mile of rough track brings you to Llyn Idwal, a spot so perfect in its symmetry and air of solitude that it seems designed for gods, not men. If asked to select just one spot that combines within itself the elements of scenery that most affect me, this would go straight onto the short list. The lake itself, Llyn Idwal, has that romantic air of brooding intensity that stirs, if not every soul, then the soul of the North European. I find that Wales always seems to be throwing up musical analogies, but never quite the ones that you might expect. This is not the Wales of choirs and deep-voiced harmonies, but it reminds me irresistibly of the darker tones of Sibelius. The cliffs and the scree run round the lake, sheltering it but darkening it at the same time, so that it seems less a relief in a rough and hostile land than a symbol of its deep and melancholy centre.

Llyn Idwal is a place that lingers in the memory, and it seems to me that impressions of the place first visited a quarter of a century ago are at least as strong as more recent recollections. Perhaps they are even stronger, for now the dark, mysterious lake has been labelled and docketed. A nature trail has been laid out around its shores, with little boards telling you just what you are looking at, and what its significance is within the wider scheme of things. There is a very human feeling that says that if you can put a name to something, you have also increased your understanding of it. A more elaborate theory would suggest that it is not the naming that is important in itself, but that the name is an acknowledgement that the phenomenon has a special place reserved to itself within a grand design. I was reminded of this on a recent visit to India where I found an immensely rich and varied bird life in the countryside. Yet I was dissatisfied, purely and simply because I was quite unable to put names to the various species. It was quite a while before I got round to asking myself what difference it would make to my response to a particular bird if I knew that it was a member of the crow family. Had I been an ornithologist, the difference would have been of immense importance, but to an amateur observer of the natural scene, the difference was negligible. And I have since decided much the same is true of the nature trail round Llyn Idwal. I have decided, in short, that I am just too ignorant to profit from it. To those who have managed to retain even a smattering of knowledge collected during botany and biology lessons at school, the notice-boards were clearly of immense value. They set the features of the land within an accepted framework of knowledge. My problem is that I lack the framework, and I do wonder if an ignoramus such as myself gains a great deal from learning the genus of a particular flower. I suspect not, and that we are just pandering to the very old notion that once we have given something a name we can begin to exercise control over it.

Information has, in any case, little to do with the appeal of this dark lake set among darker mountains. A rough, rocky path leads southwards along the shore, beneath the Idwal slabs which, in sunlight, can glow as if alive, but on a dank and misty day merely stream and steam. Everything seemed pervaded with an air of great solemnity which, given the history of the place, seems altogether appropriate. Here it was said that Nefydd the Handsome, and with a vainglorious name such as that what could he be but a wicked uncle, drowned the beautiful and good Prince Idwal. So, by this deed, the lake was cursed with barrenness. Nothing, it was said, would grow on the shore, no birds would settle on its waters nor sing on its borders. The curse was not entirely effective, yet the overriding effect of Cwm Idwal is of a gaunt and barren place. Some find this spot, with its

Snowdon: the view from the summit.

morbid legend, to be a little too forbidding, while others become fascinated. I would certainly count myself among the latter. No one could call it a cheery spot, but we all have moods when an area such as this can touch us in a very specific way. It is a very different sort of response from the uplift of the spirit you might feel on going out on a spring morning to find that the skeletal trees have quite suddenly been draped in a misty cover of opening buds. Here all is dark solemnity and austerity, yet I feel a curious intimacy with the land precisely because it offers so little in the way of instant gratification. Here is a landscape that you have to work hard at if you are to come to an understanding of it, which is the most you can hope for – you will certainly never overcome it.

On a grey, rather bleak and damp day I felt even less inclined than usual to take the place for granted. The melancholy that is an essential element in the character of Cwm Idwal was intensified, so that it seemed only sensible to accept that as the mood of the day and see where it would take you. On a dark day, what better place to go to

Llyn Gwynant.

drink in to the full this unique atmosphere than to the darkest spot in the dark land – Twll Du, the Devil's Kitchen. The name Devil's Kitchen is said to derive from the notion that the bad weather which can – and when I visit always does – afflict the area is brewed up here. The Welsh name is less fanciful, but an excellent terse description of the place, the Black Pit. For that is precisely what it is, a 250-ft-high gash struck deep into the cliff face. The path up to it leads along the eastern shore of Llyn Idwal. Rising up above at a gentle angle – gentle that is to the rock climber – are the Idwal Slabs, and generations of climbers have marked out the various routes, as their feet have worn away and polished the rock on every foothold. This is the ideal ground for beginners, and the principal routes have the encouraging names of Faith, Hope and Charity. I felt that all these elements were brought in on the first occasion I came here, for I started up in good faith, was soon hoping that I was going to reach the top in safety, and ended by wishing that my companions would take a charitable view of my rather pitiful efforts. That, however, was a long time before a busy life in London and family demands took me away from rock climbing altogether. It would be possible, though not easy, to return, but the world of climbing has changed so much that I no longer feel the urge to get back to it, and I stick to walking and scrambling. At least I tell myself I have no wish to get back to it, but the sight of a party of schoolchildren being given their first lessons on the slabs certainly twanged a few old chords.

From the end of the lake the track swings westward across the scree, a track so well used that there are none of the problems of slipping and sliding that can make moving across loose scree such a tiring occupation. As you move upwards the cliffs begin to loom above you and Twll Du itself begins to look positively menacing. One could quite sympathize with the snark hunters of Lewis Carroll's poem when they reached their destination:

> But the danger was past – they had landed at last,
> With their boxes, portmanteaus, and bags:
> Yet at first sight the crew were not pleased with the view,
> Which consisted of chasms and crags.

Chasms and crags are precisely what confront you on this dark, north-facing slope, and many find it unpleasant. But it is impressive. As the actual cleft gets closer, it becomes even more oppressive, and very forbidding. And when you finally arrive at the place itself, the effect is almost overwhelming. If ever you are going to feel that you have reached a totally wild spot, it is here. Beneath your feet it is a cascade of broken rock, above the darkness of the Devil's Kitchen. Inside the cleft is wet and dripping, slicing deep into the mountain. The waterfall at the very top provides the only sounds that reach into the deep recess until you arrive with the disturbing hollow clatter of boots on loose stones. In the cold and the damp, plants grow, but seem to be of an unnatural and unhealthy green, unnatural because it literally does seem to run contrary to the laws of nature for anything to grow in such a place. Those prepared to put up with a good wetting can penetrate quite a way into the cleft, but only the properly equipped and experienced climber can actually get to the top. I sometimes wonder why, when there are so many open, airy crags all around, anyone should want to spend their time heaving themselves up these dark and dripping walls. But, like everything else in climbing, it is a matter of accepting the natural challenge. In fact, the first ascent was quite remarkable in that it was made in the winter of 1895. The pioneers, uncertain of their chances on the walls of the cavern, borrowed an axe previously used for hacking up coal at nearby Ogwen Cottage, and used it to cut steps up the frozen waterfall.

It is possible to scramble round Twll Du to reach the summit on a narrow path to the north which is quite definitely not recommended to sufferers from vertigo, but a much wider, if longer and far rougher, track can be taken to the top. It is hard going, but eases near the summit of Clogwyn y Geifs, marked by a lake, known as Llyn y Cwn or Lake of the Dogs, for no reason that I have ever been able to discover. From here it is possible to continue on to the summit of Glyder Fawr, but the weather seemed to be getting worse and I thought it wiser to retrace my steps. This is a descent that needs to be treated with extreme caution, not because it is inherently difficult, but because it is all too easy to set off in the wrong direction – and there are precipices waiting for the unwary. The Devil's Kitchen has had its share of victims over the years and, in the majority of cases, the accidents have happened during descents. I had no wish to add to the statistics.

Tramping back through the rain, not having achieved what you set out to achieve, can be a demoralizing experience. The damp and cold you were prepared to ignore, while there was that distant objective to strive towards, now seem far more oppressive. And the prospects of dry clothes and a hot meal seem too far ahead for comfort. Water streamed over the rocks, making it all the more necessary to take care. The steep descent was turning the legs into shock-absorbers, a series of jolts replacing the steady ache of the uphill climb. Though I have never liked the notion of chair lifts and such to carry me up a mountain, I have often felt I would welcome some aid to help me down. The appeal of walking in truly wild country seemed to be slowly diminishing, as I brooded over the fact that I seemed destined never to see the hills of North Wales in the sunlight. The much

admired panorama of Tryfan and the Glyders, the distant view of *Snowdon from the west.*
Snowdon, had once again been lost under cloud. But grand views are
not the only things that bring you to the mountains – if that was all
that mattered, then you might just as well cover the whole lot with
lifts and railways. I also come to get a perspective on life, and a dark
day such as this provides the ideal environment. You soon realize that
you are in such a place on sufferance, a poor little two-legged creature
doing his best in a very large world. And with that I had to be content
as I came down off the mountain and headed for home.

We think of wild places as being unchanging, except in the sense that, like everywhere else on earth, they are subjected to those geological changes that are measured in thousands and even millions of years. Yet in East Anglia you meet a quite different type of wilderness, where changes have been compressed into a very short time span and have even, on occasion, been quite sudden and dramatic. And the period of change is not yet over – you could call this chapter a story of wilderness lost and wilderness regained. The Breckland is an extraordinary area which became for a time Britain's only desert. Two thousand years ago this was a heavily forested region, but the Saxons who came here in the fourth century began to hack down the woodland for timber, and to clear more and more of the forest away to open up the land to agriculture. Steadily but surely the forest area shrank and the land became a patchwork of open fields. But the trees had fulfilled a very special function in the land, providing protection from the strong prevailing east winds. Cover gone, the winds blew freely over the land, steadily removing the thin soil. Then, somewhere around the beginning of the fourteenth century, there was a total disaster. A huge sandstorm blew up from the east, and when the storm was finally ended the farmlands had disappeared beneath as much as three feet of sand. The old life of the area was dead, villages were abandoned, and a whole new landscape was created – the Breckland.

The new landscape represented a disaster for the farmers, but a wonderful opportunity for the local rabbit population which colonized the whole area. It became a vast warren and the local bigwigs soon hacked it up into their private preserves to take advantage of the proliferating source of rabbit pies. The result can be seen today principally in place names – Thetford Warren, Downham Highlodge Warren, Santon Warren and so on. There is also physical evidence of the importance landowners attached to the newly acquired territory. Two miles west of Thetford, in the heart of Thetford Warren, stands Warren Lodge. It looks quite unlike one's usual notion of a lodge, and rather more like a miniature fortress. And this, in a way, is just what it was, for it was home to the Warrener, the gamekeeper for the Prior of Thetford. The fortification was very necessary for his protection, which gives some idea of local opinion about the appropriation of what had been village land before the great sand blow came.

Something of the nature of the Breckland and the village life that preceded it can be gleaned at West Stow, where archaeologists found the remains of a Saxon village, fossilized as it were beneath the sand, and set about restoring it. Now you can see the village as it would have been before the catastrophe, but all around is the arid land that buried it. This is at the southern edge of the Breckland which has Thetford at its centre, and to the north you can discover the modern story of

Sea wall and dyke beside the Wash.

Breckland. Man has reclaimed the desert and turned it back into the forest it was before the Saxons came. The wheel has turned again, but has not quite come back to where it started. The ancient land was a land of natural forest; the new forest is very much the well-regulated plantation. Now the conifer reigns supreme, and only the occasional soaring Scots pine or a fringe of deciduous trees reminds us of what was once here.

The Forestry Commission who have transformed the land have made every effort to keep it as countryside to be enjoyed. Walks and bridlepaths cross and recross the woodland, making this a very popular area with walkers. There is still a little true Breckland left. You can get the authentic flavour at East Wretham Heath, now a nature reserve, where you can find another of the distinctive features of the area, the mere. These small ponds are of uncertain origin, but were once of immense importance in the otherwise arid land. Close together are Ring Mere, which is round, and Long Mere, which is long. Around these unimaginatively named lakes is the sand and scrub of the old heath. But where once it stretched for miles, now the forest all but surrounds it, as it surrounds all the small patches of the old breck. The wilderness has been tamed again, and as you walk through the forest paths it takes an act of great imagination to believe that this was once the barest, most desolate spot in all England.

My walk took me to the charming village of Santon Downham, which in its building displays another of the physical characteristics of the district, the abundance of flint. Most of it lies beneath the surface, but there is abundant evidence all around, for fragments of flint litter every pathway, and nodules push through the sandy soil. From the village I walked through the trees, noting not for the first time that East Anglia is not as flat as one is led to believe. The rise and fall of the land may be slight, but it is still registered by leg muscles as the route goes steadily uphill. All around were the conifers, the sunlight scarcely filtering through to the depths of the woods. You can see the effects at once on the trees themselves where the lower branches, deprived of light, are dead and bare and only the tops of the trees are green. So, at eye level, you seem to be walking through a maze of telegraph poles. Your common sense tells you that they are planted in straight rows, but the eyes cannot take in the information, for the trees run in an infinite variety of rows − at right angles to your path, and also away in a whole series of diagonals, a complex world of diminishing perspectives. It gives the unnerving impression that the forest goes on for ever. The forest walks are popular, but I find the experience of enveloping orderliness somewhat depressing. At least it makes you especially glad to welcome the anarchy of birdsong among the trees. Woodpigeons coo out their endless hollow calls. Somewhere a woodpecker rattles away, and coming through all the sounds is the extraordinary rasping mixture of croaks and creaks produced by the woodcock.

In the forest you can capture a little of the spirit of the Breckland but not, alas, very much. It seems that this is a land that has been finally tamed, and visitors are now carefully shepherded along the paths – red blobs on trees for pedestrians, white horseshoes to mark bridleways. But this part of the world does have one surprise left, a place where I once found myself as completely isolated and insulated from the modern world as I have ever been. A mile and a half from Santon Downham, the forest boundary is reached and you can look out across heathland, pitted and scarred with deep hollows and surrounding mounds. This is Grimes Graves.

Before the Saxons farmed here, long before the sands blew, neolithic man arrived to hunt for high-quality flint to shape into axes,

Flat fields and wide horizons.

arrowheads and spears. To reach the flint he was forced to sink pits and then burrow out from the pit bottom in a labyrinth of low, narrow tunnels. One of these pits has been opened to visitors, who can climb down a vertical ladder to peer into the illuminated passages where the miners worked four thousand years ago. It is an interesting place to visit. Above ground an excellent display explains the history and significance of the site, and the open pits provide a glimpse into the reality of the past. But this is only one of hundreds of pits, mostly, if not all, filled in. I was fortunate enough, a few years ago, to explore one of the pits that have not been tidied up for the general public. Going down the main pit is no different from going down the generally open pit, but when I reached the bottom I was able to explore the passageways. This involved a good deal of crawling on the belly and squeezing through very narrow openings. Soon the little light that comes in from the top of the main shaft is just a memory, and the only light you have is what you bring with you.

I had crawled to a point where work had been abandoned. The old flint miners had excavated a sort of circular cave 3 feet high and had exposed the flint at floor level, where it occurs as a wide band in the chalk. They had continued chipping away at the chalk, using deer antlers as pick axes, when the wall gave way and they found that they had broken through into an old, abandoned working. There was no point in going on, so they left and the hole in the wall was left as well. Through that hole you can still see the workings undisturbed since work ended thousands of years ago. The old antler picks lie beside the face, surrounded by the rubble of chalk dug out by the miners. It is a curious sensation to stare through to that other world, which is what I was doing when the light went out. Darkness came down like a velvet hood. Of course, I was not alone in the excavations and I could, in any case, have found my way out by feeling my way back down the passageways, though only at the expense, no doubt, of a few scrapes and bruises. So I waited, and during the wait I sat in that total, impenetrable blackness, surrounded by the memories of the men who had toiled here in the so distant past. If there were ghosts here, none returned to haunt me, in fact I felt curiously comfortable in the dark cave. It is a very special sensation to be closed up like that within the heart of the earth. If my imagination had failed me when I tried to conjure up images of the old Breckland, it certainly did not fail me then. I really felt I could understand something of what it must have meant to men with such primitive equipment to create this underground world: the reason for placing a little votive offering at the foot of the pit as a charm. But equally I felt that these men had been true masters of their underground domain. I was alone under the earth, for a while, and I can only describe it as a friendly place. Then the lights came, and I could return to the surface. The memory of that solitary wait in the neolithic mine remains as vivid as ever. If this was not, in the strict sense, a wilderness, then it was certainly a place where I felt that I had come to a new understanding of one aspect of the natural world.

The Breckland adjoins another region where the nature of the land has been dramatically changed by man's intervention – the Fens. Once this whole area of East Anglia was a vast swamp of marshy land, through which sluggish rivers made their tortuous way. Islands of drier land rose up above the level plain to form centres of settlement, centres that remain visible landmarks for many miles, mainly because of the marks man has added – the towers of Ely Cathedral or the Boston Stump.

For a long time this was thought of as a trackless, all but impenetrable, wasteland until aerial photography revealed straight lines ruled across the fens, joining the drier margins to the islands. At first it seemed incredible to believe that in ancient times any sort of track could ever have been constructed in such an inhospitable region, let alone a network as complex as the photographs suggested. And if this really was an ancient communications system, then what form could such tracks possibly take? Much work remains to be done before any positive answers can be provided for the fens, but excavations in a very similar area give us an idea of what to expect. The Somerset Levels had precisely the same pattern of islands in a boggy sea before modern drainage works changed the landscape. Here too were the same straight-lined tracks, and here the archaeologists found their evidence. The earliest routes turned out to be pathways formed out of brushwood hurdles pegged into the peaty ground. These date back to 3,000 BC, while a thousand years later even more elaborate causeways of split logs and planks were constructed. There seems to be every reason to suppose that the fenland tracks are of equal antiquity – and somehow this evidence has to be keyed into the fascinating geological history of the region.

At first the story seems simple, one of flat lands formed by the silt of the inundating sea, yet beneath that silt, bog oaks are found, showing that in prehistoric times part at least was forested. But after the inundation this was a strange and lonely land, its ways known to very few, making it the ideal hiding-place for men such as Hereward the Wake. But men were changing it all the time. First of all, embankments were built against the sea. Then, when the Romans came, they began building drainage channels and over the centuries more and more channels were dug. Then those most experienced of land reclaimers, the Dutch, came across with their pumps powered by windmills. So the land constantly changed. The silt formed a rich, black soil, but elsewhere rotting vegetation had left a thick layer of peat. And as the continuous drainage sucked the water from the peat, so the land fell, dropping as much as an inch a year.

The old fenland of reed and sedge, rich with wildfowl, began to disappear, and with it the life of the region changed as well. Those who had made a living from the old land now had to adapt to the new world of the settled farmer. By the end of the nineteenth century the fenland had all but vanished – almost but not quite. It would all have gone, too, had not one little area been discovered by naturalists hunting for rare species of butterfly. They viewed with alarm the prospect of this last natural habitat, this final remnant of undrained land, going the way of the rest of the fens. Wind pump and steam pump were sucking the land dry, and they determined that Wicken Fen at least would be kept wet. They began to buy it up and, in 1899, part of the fen came under the ownership of the National Trust and became established as the country's first nature reserve. The reserve now covers an area of some 700 acres, a reasonably large stretch of

On the edge of the Wash near to Holbeach St Matthew.

land it seems, until you remember that the Great Fen once covered 2,500 square miles. Small it may be, but Wicken Fen is now a splendid wilderness in miniature.

The National Trust area consists of the fen itself, together with an area to the south, Adventurers Fen, which was turned over to agriculture during the 1939–45 war, but has now returned to wasteland, an attractive spot for visiting birds. It is also very popular with ornithologists, but that reclamation has destroyed the essential nature of the fen, which is so much in evidence at Wicken Fen itself. It is a character that is unique, which makes it difficult to describe for it lacks familiar reference points. Arriving by car, you turn off the main road, park, walk a few yards and there it is.

I am told that Wicken Fen is a popular spot, but not, it appears, on a wet, cold Sunday when the calendar declares that spring has arrived but someone forgot to tell the weather. The only other person I met was the warden out walking his domain with two very waterlogged spaniels, looking thoroughly miserable and not managing a tail wag between the pair of them. On the whole, though, I considered myself quite fortunate since I have never minded the rain. I was quite happy to put up with a little dampness if it meant that I could have the place to myself, and in any case the rain seemed to fit in well enough with the atmosphere. I did not, of course, really have the place to myself, for though there were no other human beings around, there was no shortage of life. The air was alive with the call of birds, and I could see them on every hand. There were all kinds and varieties of them – flying, walking, swimming birds; birds that sang sweet melodies and birds that rasped and hooted. A small booklet provided by the Wicken Fen Group, formed in 1968 to study the bird life, informed me that 37,000 birds were ringed here in fifteen years, covering eighty different species. The list is wonderfully impressive and even records the presence of a few exotics, refugees from their domestic prisons seeking sanctuary on the fen. It seems unlikely, however, that the budgerigars, canaries and cockatoos will ever find a true home among the native population. It is the birds that bring the visitors, but there is a lot more to Wicken Fen than ornithology.

You can quickly become accustomed, after the initial surprise, to finding that the noise of traffic on the nearby road is drowned by the clamour of birdsong, but the visual shock is far greater. The fen really does carry that extraordinary air of being a place scarcely touched by the centuries. It is not colourful, and the general effect is rather that of seeing an old sepia print than that of any reality. The overwhelming first impression is of a world of dull reed and sedge. The latter is one of those plants of which everyone has heard, but which few can recall actually seeing – or, if they did see it, they had no idea what they were looking at. That best known of couplets, learned by generations of schoolchildren:

> The sedge is wither'd from the lake,
> And no birds sing

appears at least half appropriate here. Birds sing in profusion, but the sedge itself has precisely that dried-up appearance that Keats's lines suggest. It rustles drily in the wind, forming a waving fringe to the wet area which appears as a shining grey in the grey light, an area of soft beauty, speckled with the drifting wakes of waterfowl. At the edge stands the little wind pump from Adventurers Fen in sombre black, with its small scoop wheel still attached. If it had ever been set to work here, Wicken Fen would have been irrevocably lost. As it is, you can walk around the perimeter and see just how, imperceptible as it might appear at first, man has altered this apparently natural environment.

Near the tiny windmill are the remains of brick pits, where the grey, slimy clay that streaks the black of the squelchy peat has been dug out and sent to the brickyards. Now the pits are water-filled, and are home to a rich variety of water plants. It is a comfort to find that man's interference with the land can so quickly seem to become a part of the natural order again, and can even increase the richness and variety of the natural plant life of the area. The same story is repeated as you make your way around the increasingly slippery path on the eastern edge of the fen. The so natural-seeming willows have, in fact, grown up from abandoned fence posts. At this point there is an obviously artificial grassed pathway through the trees. This is sedge fen drove and is no innovation at Wicken, for it has been used for three centuries by generations of local men who came to cut reed and sedge. It forms one of the few open tracts in this part of the fen, for elsewhere there is a thick and all-but impenetrable blackthorn thicket. Within its depths unseen birds call, the one distinguishable sound being the staccato tap of the woodpecker. A pathway exists through the thicket, but being the only pathway it is comparatively well used and in this wet season had become a cloying quagmire. I slopped through for a way, but it was clearly impassable. With some reluctance I turned back, not liking to admit defeat.

I set off again to try my luck around the southern edge, where an invitingly broad path leads between the fen and Wicken Lode, the waterway which was used to take drainage water from the land to the east off into the River Cam. In its time it was regularly used by working boats, part of a whole complex of navigable drains that carve through East Anglia. In fact, until I made the acquaintance of Wicken Fen. I would have said to anybody who expressed the urge to be alone with the great expanses of the flat lands, that there was no better way than to travel by boat. Few bother to explore the drains, for they are mostly cut off from the rest of the world behind high banks or else emerge into a no-man's-land of wind-bent reeds. And it is possible to combine the two experiences by coming here by boat down the Wicken Lode.

For the time being I was left with a still squelchy but quite comfortable walk. Breaks in the trees revealed the open views across the waving fringe of sedge. The sedge is cut every four years to be used for thatching, and to ensure its survival in good condition, and the fen itself occasionally has to have the water level raised by pumping. It seemed unlikely that such action would be needed for some time. It is one of the features of the fen, that although it remains an essentially wild environment it exists within a cultivated land, and if the wilderness is to be preserved, then notice has to be taken of what is going on all around. As if to emphasize that this is now an artificially preserved wilderness, kept to serve special purposes, the view round the next corner of woodland revealed a tall wooden tower. This is the hide for bird watchers, a place where the enthusiasts will sit for hours, seeing but unseen. It is an artificial structure, but without it man would find it that much more difficult to understand the natural world beyond the tower. It offers fine views, they say, and on a clear day you can see Newmarket racecourse. On this particular day it was all I could do to peer through the rain to see the edge of the fen. That at

The reed beds of Wicken fen.

least preserved me from feeling that sense of inferiority which usually accompanies my visit to such places. All around me the birds were busy getting on with their lives, and I had little idea of what most of them were or what they were doing. But there was no one at my elbow, peering through binoculars, identifying species and providing an expert running commentary on the antics of the wildfowl. I accept that the experts will probably get more out of the place than I ever shall, but I was glad for once to be left alone. Sometimes I feel that I have no interest in understanding a place through the activity of the brain: I would rather let it announce itself through the senses. This was just such a day. The atmosphere of this small piece of preserved fenland was so strong that I had no wish to intellectualize it. Here in this wet, dripping world of grey water and gently rustling reeds I felt that I had arrived at a genuine wild spot, a piece of the wilderness which had stories to tell of this land before it was tamed. I was content with that. There was something especially appealing about the notion that this wilderness existed so close to the other tamed and cultivated world of East Anglia. That same feeling was to be repeated with even greater force when I left Wicken Fen for a tramp along the northern edge of the region.

All the way to the Wash, the landscape is dominated by the huge flat fields which in spring become transformed by the blossoming flowers into a patchwork of colour. Crowds come in to admire, but for the rest of the year it is a dead land, with scarcely a person moving. My wife and I came in the dead days between winter and spring, when the daffodils were finished and the rest of the flowers were still to come. The colour-scheme of the land really is like army camouflage, the rich, dark browns of newly ploughed fields alternating with the depleted greenery of the daffodil fields. Only a few flowers remained, brave little yellow flags fluttering in a vicious north wind. To me it has always seemed one of the most alien landscapes in all Britain. Houses have been plonked down at the intersection of the ruled lines of field boundaries and roads, as plain and dull as a child's first efforts with building blocks. They have no sense of permanence, no feeling of belonging, and time and the elements seem to have done little enough to mellow them. They look as if they are there by mistake and retained on sufferance, and so in a sense they are. For if man were to relax his vigilance and let fall his defences, the sea would reclaim them all.

It is easy to imagine the land being lost again, for it has so little personality to lose – no hedges, no fences, no walls, no copses, just fields: plain, unadorned fields. The only decorative elements you can find are the curlicues and scrolls cut at the field edges by the turning plough. There is a dull conformity to the land which I find quite unappealing. But all that ends at the sea wall, the great earthwork that separates the cultivated land from the marshes and the encroaching sea.

We set out from Gedney Drove End to walk across the fields to the sea wall. As at Wicken Fen, it is the birdsong that instantly bombards the senses. Gulls wheel and mew much as they do in any area that borders the sea, but other more surprising calls also cut the air. A skylark hangs above a field, endlessly trilling. Ducks quack across the horizon, looking absurdly like parlour-wall plaster casts as they take up formation. And, most surprisingly, a fat pheasant rises up from underfoot to skim the surface of the field with loud complaint. Then, as we turned towards the sea itself along a farm track, a labrador appeared and appended himself to the party. No amount of declaring 'home, boy', no pointed finger made the least impression upon him. Visitors, and visitors off for a walk, represented an opportunity not to be missed. He was going to join us whether we liked it or not. And he certainly enjoyed himself: not a smell along the way was left unsniffed, not a post unmarked and not a single, muddy puddle was circumvented. If he was in training for the title 'scruffiest dog of the year' then, by the end of the walk, he looked every grimy inch the winner. And all the way his tail never stopped wagging.

As we reached the top of the sea wall the divisions in the land became plain. On one side were the fields and reclaimed land, on the other the untouched marshes. It is only with a certain amount of trepidation that any stranger ventures onto the seaward side of the wall. Large notices warn of the dangers from the creeks and tides. The map shows danger areas where the RAF practise bombing. And the local wildfowlers are frequently out in force, and even when they are not on view the evidence of their activity is plainly visible in heaps of red and blue cartridge shells. Those prepared to risk tide, bombs and bullets are rewarded, however, with a strange solitary stretch of coastline, quite unlike anything else in Britain. The land itself is a jigsaw, the pieces defined by the creeks that slide and sidle through the turf, twisting in every direction. Gistening mud banks act as reminders that these are indeed tidal waterways and that what can seem a harmless grassland cut by streams at low tide can be transformed with amazing rapidity as the tide starts to come in. It is a very different land from that sheltering behind the bank. Different plants grow here, short grasses and marsh dwellers. And the consistency of the ground seems to change all the time as well, from springy dry turf to treacherous, cloying bogs.

This area is also unlike any other I know in that the main drama does not take place on the earth at all. It is not what you see beneath your feet that creates the atmosphere. There is, it is true, a strangeness about the conventional view. If you look out towards the sea you could believe yourself lost in the most desolate spot on earth, for

Wicken fen.

nothing occurs to disturb the horizon, apart from a distant lump of an island out in the Wash. Turn round, however, and the sea wall rules an immense line on the map, defining the beginning of man's domain and the end of the wild lands. And you can walk all day, battering against the biting wind, and the divisions will remain the same, and you will never quite lose your awareness of man's impositions on the landscape. This, of all places I have visited, is the one where walking makes very little difference to your initial perception of the landscape. The secret, if you want to find the special factor, is to stop, be still and look neither outwards, nor down, but up. The skies are the chief glory of East Anglia. Elsewhere buildings, hills, trees and all manner of obstructions may block out the view, but there the whole dome of the sky can be seen from horizon to horizon, no matter which way you turn.

The patterns of the sky are never still, and on a day of high winds the movements are rapid and continual. Platoons of clouds march upwards from one horizon in an endless perspective like chorus girls in a Busby Berkeley movie. They march on overhead and then stride on down the slope of the sky to disappear again. Individualistic clouds wheel away from the main squad to perform solos, capering for a while on the edge of the regimented rows, before bowing to the demands of discipline and rejoining the ranks. And beneath this march past of the clouds, the air is scarcely less busy. A marsh harrier hovers with difficulty, wings working hard to keep on station in the face of the gale. Smaller birds scurry low above the ground, keeping up a continuous conversational chatter. And looking out towards the North Sea, it is still the sky that dominates, endless movements reflected on still waters. Looking upwards, it is not hard to see how we came to perceive ourselves as standing at the still centre of a revolving universe. It is the infinity of the sky that seems to be in perpetual motion, while we remain fixed points, focus of it all.

It would be easy on a fine summer's day simply to sit and let this whole airy world pivot around you. But stillness and a keen north wind do not go well together. We walked back from the marshes to the dividing bank and our north-bound route. Man's additions to this weird landscape do little to enhance it. Orange markers for the bombing ranges fit uneasily into the sombre colours, while up ahead the outline of the detention centre adds a less than cheery note. But, being a bookish sort of person, it did act as a trigger to the imagination. I remembered another marsh and the encounter between Pip and the convict Magwitch in *Great Expectations*. And the marsh certainly looked less grim than the wire and watchtowers of the detention centre.

As you walk, or rather fight, against the wind, you do after a while begin to wonder why you are making the effort. The scene changes

Beyond the sea wall:
the marshland of the Wash.

very little, certainly not as rapidly as your own body temperature which gets colder by the minute. With no shelter on offer, there is not much joy to be had from standing still, so the sensible thing seemed to be to turn for home. It was after taking that decision that I discovered one of life's rich pleasures: turning away from a leaning walk into an icy north wind to receive the same wind in your back to send you happily bounding back towards thoughts of comfort. On this occasion, comfort appeared in the shape of a friendly pub with decent grub and a splendid pint of Adnam's bitter – and bitters do not come a great deal more splendid than that. I also had a chance to reflect on the fact that I had learned something else about my own attitudes. I can see the attractions of these wild, open lands of the east coast. I understand the appeal, yet I have to admit that it never touches me in the way that the first sight of hill country can always do. It is, I suppose, largely habit, a question of where one was brought up, but I know I shall always find a far keener pleasure in the hills. I was glad to have been to East Anglia, had found much to enjoy and in Wicken Fen had found a hauntingly beautiful spot which I had not expected. But, for all that, I shall not be rushing back. The fault, if it is a fault rather than a simple lack of perception, lies entirely with me, but I think it lies too deep to be eradicated. If some people are hill people and others feel they belong on the plains, then I have no doubt where my allegiance lies.

Arbor Low stone circle.

8. THE PEAK DISTRICT

Derbyshire is a splendid county, full of variety and fascination. Over the years I have stomped across many a mile of it, finding special satisfaction in being able to combine my interest in industrial history with fine hill walking. It was here that I began walking the routes of long-disused railways, and if that conjures up images of marching along dull, straight lines then you have never encountered a railway like the Cromford and High Peak. It was described rather neatly by a nineteenth-century travel writer: 'The skyscraping High Peak Railway with its corkscrew curves that seem to have been laid out by a mad Archimedes endeavouring to square the circle.' It starts beside the canal that runs from the world's first cotton mill at Cromford – you can now see perhaps something of its special appeal to the author. Here it is at an altitude of 277 feet, but in its climb across the Pennines on the southern edge of the Peak District it reaches a height of 1,264 feet before dropping down again to 517 feet. This remarkable feat was accomplished by means of a series of inclined planes, steep slopes up which trains were hauled by cables worked by steam engines at the top. Engine-house and engine can still be seen at the top of the Middleton incline.

There is, however, no need to have even the least interest in railways, steam engines and the like to enjoy walking the route, which is now officially known as the High Peak Trail. Starting at the Cromford end, you climb straight up towards Cromford Moor, overlooked by a typical Derbyshire gritstone outcrop – the Black Rocks. They stand high above the surrounding trees, gaining their rather grim-sounding name from the fact that the crags face north and are so in constant shadow. At close range the rough, rounded stones can be seen to have the lighter tinges of sandstone. The rocks are a prominent landmark, popular with climbers who have set out a maze of routes of varying degrees of difficulty and complexity, but they are equally accessible to those of more modest ambitions. From the top you get a splendid view over to Matlock and the Derwent valley, though I can well remember one particular morning when mist lapped at the foot of the crags and only the more distant peaks rose above the white sea. It was as if I had stepped into a Japanese painting of great subtlety and delicacy.

The railway route continues to follow a lonely line across the moors, skirting quarries, twisting round the southern outskirts of Buxton before heading northwards up the Goyt valley – and what a splendid place that is – to its final destination at Whaley Bridge. Here what remains of the track disappears into a large, stone building, and the route re-emerges at the opposite end of the same building, transfigured into water as the Peak Forest Canal. In recent years the route has become very popular with walkers, who have found it an excellent way of spending a weekend. Cromford and Whaley Bridge are just 25 miles apart, but the splendid old corkscrew railway transforms it into a 33-mile journey. I have often asked myself whether I would enjoy the walk as much if it were just a walk, and I have to admit that I would not. I would certainly still enjoy it, for the scenery and the walking are excellent throughout – but I would not enjoy it as much. For me, one of the appeals of Derbyshire lies in combining walking with the investigation of the past. And few areas can boast a richer past than this. You can look out for the lead mines, which have been worked since Roman times, the underground exploration of which combines historical fieldwork with the excitements of caving. Old mills turn up in remote valleys, and the railways run through the lot. Many of the latter have been abandoned and, like the High Peak, have been transformed into routes for walkers and, in some cases, cyclists. They stretch across the county border into Staffordshire and, in one case, provided a surprising encounter.

Lady Clough Moor to the north of Kinder Scout.

A couple of years ago my wife and I stayed at a pub then called The Light Railway which once served the adjoining Leek and Manifold which gave it its name. The walk along the line is quite undemanding, but half-way along is one of the most spectacular natural phenomona of the area – Thor's Cave. The cavern can be seen near the top of the hill, 250 feet above the valley floor. The opening is remarkable, for it is an almost circular hole worn in the limestone, 23 feet wide and 30 feet high. Not surprisingly, a great many stories and legends surround the place, but you do not expect to meet any mythical or mystical characters on a bright and sunny morning. But as we climbed the hill we looked up and saw coloured fumes belch from the mouth. A strange, helmeted figure raised his dark cloak like the wings of a bat and disappeared into the opening. The explanation for this weird sight was predictably mundane. It had nothing to do with ghosts and legends, except in a commercial sense. A film company were at work

Kinder Scout from Hayfield.

on an epic, and Thor's Cave was, for the day, the dragon's lair. My mysterious figure in the cloak was a little man with a smudge of a moustache, standing in for the star who presumably had his own feet up back at the hotel. Far away on the opposite hill were the camera crew, and inside the cave were the technicians in charge of pyrotechnics. We were simply a nuisance and were politely asked to stay inside the cave until the next shot was completed. This was no great hardship, for the cave is a truly amazing place with a giant pillar supporting the roof and a rock floor that slopes vertiginously away towards the valley and the distant hills. Such experiences cannot be guaranteed as part of the pleasures of walking the old railways, but I still find the lines a most satisfactory way of seeing the country.

Industry in some form or other pervades Derbyshire, hill and valley alike, but has never diminished the appeal of the wilder places. But there is also another aspect to the country: there is the Derbyshire of the big landowners. Here you can find some of the finest stately homes in Britain – Haddon Hall, Hardwick Hall, Kedleston Hall and, greatest of them all, Chatsworth. The owners decorated their houses with carvings and paintings, surrounded them by splendid parks and, in general, did all they could to beautify and aggrandize their homes. All this would have had little to do with those who look mainly to get away from the luxuries of life in favour of the more spartan pleasures of the hills, were it not for the fact that the owners of these estates had their own favoured way of enjoying the countryside. They shot – and still shoot – birds. In particular, they shoot grouse and the grouse live on the moors. This was not a problem to the wealthy, who simply appropriated the moors, appointed gamekeepers to look after the birds and kept the rest of the population away. And in this they succeeded for a very long time. It was an arrangement that suited the sporting landowner very well. It was presumably looked upon less favourably by the grouse and, in the twentieth century, it came to be regarded with great distaste by the debarred common man. There was, as current jargon would have it, a conflict situation – or, in plain English, there were two sides ready to do battle. They clashed on 25 April 1932 on Kinder Scout.

The argument itself seemed simple enough, the difficulties arose partly because the argument varied a good deal, depending on where you were standing in the first place and also because there was, from the first, a political element. To one side, the issue was that of a privileged few trying to preserve a wide expanse of the finest open countryside for their own limited use. To the others it was a question of not allowing a rag-bag of people, many of whom came from the surrounding industrial towns, to disrupt a long-established part of country life. It was also seen in class terms: common man against landlord, proletariat against aristocrat. Emotions seemed at least as important as rational argument, and the emotions have survived for half a century. This became very obvious in 1982, when on the fiftieth anniversary of the confrontation participants came forward to give their version of what had happened on that April day. Each told different versions of what they clearly regarded as the absolute truth, but from the various accounts some basic facts can be recited.

On that morning a body of people, estimates varying from two hundred to about six hundred, set out on a walk that involved a deliberate act of trespass on the private grouse moor of Kinder Scout. They were met by a body of gamekeepers, there were some scuffles, but nothing very serious, and a number of arrests. On these few points all agree. Beyond that, all is argument and muddle. Were the walkers country enthusiasts demanding their rights of access to the country-side or were they communist agitators trying to score political points? Were the gamekeepers protectors of money and privilege prepared to use any means to keep the moors as the preserve of the rich, or were they conservationists trying to keep the true life of the country intact from would-be exploiters. Did those who decided to engage in the mass trespass of Kinder Scout really penetrate to the heart of the moorland, establishing the rights of everyone to have reasonable access to the countryside or were they repulsed by a brave band of heavily outnumbered keepers? It is difficult now to disentangle the conflicting accounts. It is equally difficult to assess the importance of the walk. One side claims that reasonable concessions and access were always available to all genuine hill walkers, others that without the dramatic demonstration of public determination, the moors would still be closed. Those who were there that day are as far from agreement as ever.

Today, Kinder Scout is open to the public and, in fact, the first and greatest of the long-distance footpaths, the Pennine Way, begins with the ascent of the hill from Edale. The sight of so many walkers heading towards Kinder Downfall, the ultimate goal of the 1932 trespass, must gladden the heart of the surviving law-breakers. The gamekeepers are perhaps less well pleased, as they try to protect the young grouse through the late spring and early summer, preparing them for the Glorious Twelfth when the crack of shotguns is still heard on the moor. The grouse have still to give an opinion.

Kinder Scout is not, however, quite the hill it was fifty years ago. The very popularity of the Pennine Way has changed the atmosphere of the place, making it, in summer, as busy as any hill in the country. There have been physical changes as well, for the old pathways have become wide, eroded tracks. Yet in spite of the changes, Kinder retains a unique character among our hills, a character that might best be described as slightly surly. No one would, I think, describe this as a welcoming environment, but then you cannot order the land to rearrange itself for your personal preference, so you have to take Kinder Scout as you find it – which is mainly dark, waterlogged and sombre of mood.

Edale is as good a place as any to start for an ascent of Kinder, if only because it typifies so many of the Derbyshire Dales. It runs roughly in an east–west direction, a narrow vale closely hemmed in by hills. Small farms surrounded by a maze of stone walls dot the lower slopes, and it seems the epitome of rural peace and quiet. Nothing you feel can have changed here for centuries, just a continuity of farm life, apart from the brief eruption of the trespass. But Derbyshire would not be Derbyshire if my other theme were not being played here as well. The Industrial Revolution reached out into this mountain valley in the 1790s. It was in Derbyshire twenty years earlier that Richard Arkwright established his first successful cotton mill, and other mills were soon established throughout the region. They were all initially powered by waterwheel and, as all regular walkers in this part of the country can testify, the Peak District is seldom short of water. In time

The aptly named Snake Pass.

the Edale mill was transformed into a steam mill, and the tall chimney still stands to proclaim the fact. It is a fine four-storey building of local stone, which the weathering of the years has done much to soften, and it has many a note of grace to please the eye. It seems now as much a part of the rural scene as the surrounding farms and cottages. It is hard to see it for what it is, a representative of that small group of buildings that ushered in the factory age and the start of the modern world – difficult to remember that it was in such buildings that women and small children worked twelve and more hours a day. That is long in the past, but the mill itself continued in use for a century and a half and was still working at the time of the Great Trespass. Yet it is not just a reminder of the past, for it is now one of the possible starting places for exploring the High Peak District. In 1969 the mill was bought by that admirable organization, the Landmark Trust, who specialize in the restoration of buildings of true character, which they then let out as holiday homes. Over the years I have become addicted to the Landmark Trust and have stayed in an extraordinary range of buildings, ranging from a coverted engine-house in Cornwall to a medieval hall in Wales. Edale Mill is slightly different because of its size, and much of it now is permanently occupied. I find it very pleasing that, as with the old railways, so the old mill has been preserved yet put to a good use in helping people to enjoy the countryside.

The difficulty with Kinder Scout lies initially in deciding which of the possible routes to tackle, for there are, not surprisingly, a variety of routes to a hill the top of which is a plateau 5 miles long and 3 miles across at the widest point. Even the Pennine Way appears in the plural. There is a direct route which runs north from the village or a simpler route further to the west. To add to the general confusion, there is officially no such village as Edale anyway. What we think of as Edale is Grindsbrook Booth, with neighbours Nether Booth and Upper Booth, below and above it. I opted to start off on the northern path of the Way, which takes you past the Nag's Head – if you can resist temptation – and the very attractive church.

The actual road ends and you are faced by the deep cleft of Grindsbrook biting into the flank of Kinder Scout. In gloomy weather it can seem a forbidding spot, a darker shadow on the already dark landscape, but on a bright summer's day it looked coolly inviting – a good deal too inviting for I had already decided, probably foolishly, to take the direct route up to the northern lip of the plateau, marked by a line of rocks that go by the splendid name of Ringing Roger. The slope itself is grassy, which helps put a little spring into the step as you toil upwards. The young and fit stride straight on towards their objective – we who are not so young and not quite so fit continue upwards by a

Edale: the southern end of the Pennine Way.

long zigzagging path which reduces the angle of the slope but doubles the distance you walk. You can always tell the physical condition of walkers such as myself by the number of times we 'stop to admire the view', which is the discreet way of pausing for breath. There is in any case every justification for stopping a while. Below you the deep cleft runs down with just a glint of light from the waters of the brook as it emerges from the shadows. Other brooks find their own way down on either side of our route, cutting their own channels or cloughs into the hill.

In early summer it is very tempting to sit down, stop worrying about other destinations and simply enjoy the scene. With luck, you will remain relatively undisturbed. In fact, such disturbances as do occur are more likely to bother the native inhabitants, the red grouse, than they are to bother you. The progress of other walkers can be mapped by the sudden flurry of the disturbed grouse which, waiting until the last minute in their cover of heather, rear up and rush noisily away, complaining about the intrusion. Judging from the number that appear in this way, the walkers have left plenty for the cartridges of the Twelfth. But tempting as it is just to sit, there is a nagging something rather like conscience that tells you that you have set out to reach the top and you should be on your way. So, breath recovered, you turn away from the view and back towards the summit which, disconcertingly, seems to have moved further away than when you stopped. So on you plod until you reach the rocks, a thousand feet above the starting-point in the village.

Now there really is a chance to take in the entire vista of the dark moor, with Grindsbrook fully in view, falling and curling away through the shadows. It tumbles off the edge of the plateau close to the gently rising ground of Grindslow Knoll. Having reached this point, you have the liberty of the high land and can set off in any direction you choose to be greeted by ever-changing views, each it seems as dramatic as the last. To the east lies a rock jumble known, for reasons which no one now seems to remember, as Madwoman's Stones. They stand near the top of one of the many streams that the guidebook describes as draining down from Kinder Scout. They are not, it appears, very efficient drains, for the top consists of permanently boggy peat which can make for very heavy going. This particular stream runs down another deep clough, known as Jaggers, and leads on to the bright waters of Ladybower Reservoir.

I turned off towards the rim of the plateau to look down towards the Snake Road, more prosaically known as the A57. The name might be thought to derive from the sinuous and serpentine progress of the road through the hills, but in fact the origin is not geographical at all. It comes from the snake that features in the coat of arms of the local landowning family, the Cavendishes. Beyond the road a tract of bare moorland rises up to the seemingly trackless waste of Bleaklow. Bleak it certainly is, but not as trackless as it seems. The Pennine Way passes across, but that is something of a newcomer, for the Romans were here centuries ago and built their road across the lower slope. From here I decided to follow the track around the rim of the plateau, which seemed far preferable to coping with the peat bogs and dark, brackish pools of the centre. But if the centre is uninviting, a place where even the vegetation seems drab and gloomy, the walk round the rim is splendid, and the views get better and better as you go on. Now the weathered gritstone begins to appear as an edge to the hill in ever-bigger outcrops. The cloughs still give a serrated margin to the land as you cross first Middle Seal Clough with its guardian stone at the top and then Fairbrook marked promisingly on the map as a waterfall, but which turned out in practice to be a very disappointing affair. Fortunately the same could not be said of Fairbrook Naze, where the line of crags mark a very definite and precise edge. A good place for lunch, the guidebook said – and I took the hint.

Suitably rested, I set off for another enticing part of the edge, where the rocky outcrops have been eroded by wind and weather into some

Lady Clough Moor.

weird and fantastical shapes. The most famous group of rocks is known as the Boxing Gloves, and for once the name does seem entirely apt, a perfect description of the two great boulders. This is, in my experience, unusual. There is scarcely an eroded stone group anywhere in the Pennines which has not been given a name of some sort, intended to be descriptive. In most cases, however, only the most vivid imagination could fit the image suggested by the name with the physical reality. The only similarity between the Cow and Calf at Ilkley, for example, and any beasts you might see in the fields comes from the fact that one rock group is bigger than the other. Fancy, however, reaches its apotheosis at Brimham Rocks where you can find the Turtle, the Druid's Writing Desk, the Dancing Bear and many more extravagantly named outcrops. Whenever I see people sagely nodding and agreeing that yes, that is indeed a most accurate representation of a druid's idol or whatever, I always think they must be blessed with more imagination than I. Or they are simply doing a Polonius.

> HAMLET   Do you see yonder cloud that's almost in shape of a camel?
> POLONIUS   By the mass and 'tis, like a camel indeed.
> HAMLET   Methinks it is like a weasel.
> POLONIUS   It is backed like a weasel.
> HAMLET   Or like a whale.
> POLONIUS   Very like a whale.

At least the Boxing Gloves are very like boxing gloves – and not the least bit like a whale. After reaching that firm decision, I turned away to pick up the well-marked Pennine Way again as it headed towards what can be the most spectacular spot on the whole of Kinder Scout, Kinder Downfall.

This is more than just a magnificent feature in the Peak District landscape: it was also the ultimate objective of the walkers in the 1930s campaign. To reach it today might seem a matter of little importance, yet fifty years ago it had a very special significance, for *hoi polloi* were denied even a sight of it. That privilege was reserved for the owners and those who were granted the favour of a passage across the private moor. As a result, one comes to it with high expectations which, sadly, at the end of a dry period, were not about to be fulfilled. This is a place of many moods. In wet weather, the Downfall reveals itself as a majestic waterfall, tumbling off the end of a rocky ledge. In winter it becomes an icy confection, a frozen, gleaming mass. It is seen as its most exciting when there is a full flow of water and the wind blows up the valley. The fall is reversed, blowing back on itself in a giant plume of water. But in dry weather it is a trickle, as exciting as a malfunctioning shower in a third-rate hotel, yet even at its lowest ebb the surrounding formations, the high rock walls, make it a spot well worth visiting. It is also the point where the walker must take a decision, weighing the attractions of scenic delights up ahead with fatigue in the leg muscles. The adventurous, still full of energy, head off again round the plateau rim to make their final descent to Edale via Grindsbrook. The weaker brethren head for a gentler route via Kinder Low, the southernmost point of the plateau. I opted for weakness, and the fastest and easiest route for home. This way is known as Jacob's Ladder: in Biblical terms this led up to Paradise. On this occasion the story was reversed, for it was the route that would take me down, if not to Paradise, then to the comforts of a hot bath, to be followed by a hot meal and cool beer. I headed back towards Upper Booth leaving others to complete the grand circuit of Kinder Scout. I really felt that there was little point in rushing to see the whole area in one day. I had been before to Kinder Scout and I shall come back again. It is a marvellous, if sombre, tract of land which has somehow got left behind between the aggressive urban developments of Yorkshire and Lancashire.

The fiftieth anniversary of the trespass certainly brought a lot of people back to the Peak District. It also brought a lot of fresh consideration of the problems posed by our wild places. It must have seemed fifty years ago that a great victory had been won: the land had been taken away from the privileged few and returned to the people. But the question of what 'the people' should do with the land still remains to be answered, even if we were sure any longer of what we mean by 'the people'. Increasingly such places seem to have become political pawns, handled by a variety of interested parties. Even the National Parks administrators seem powerless to prevent the destruction of the wilderness. Ancient buildings can, in theory at any rate, be saved from destruction by being placed under official protection. But no one, it seems, has the power to prevent the destruction of the countryside: are ancient landscapes really less important than old buildings? The Peak District is just one area under threat from ploughing, fencing and plantations. In one sense, it is worse off than it was before. At least the old landlords had no doubt about where their interests lay. The country was to be kept wild for the grouse. But those days will never return. So what should the new owners do – who indeed are the new owners? Should anyone be able to lay claim to ownership of the wild places? Until these questions have been resolved, no one can say that the battle of the moorland is over. Who knows when the next mass trespass will occur.

9. THE PENNINES

The Colne Valley.

Shepherd, sheep, dogs and dry stone walls: the working world of the Pennines.

'There is', we are frequently reminded, 'no place like home.' An ageing cliché, but, like many an old saying long past its best, it has survived so long because there is some truth in it. Nowhere will ever have quite the same magic as the land where we first discovered the beauties and appeal of the wild country. For me, this was the Pennine hills of Yorkshire, where I was brought up and where I very soon discovered that the concepts of wilderness and beauty can have many interpretations. I lived near the edge of the dales and was somewhat inclined to take the countryside for granted. But friends lived in the mill towns, and their appreciation of the country was of a different order from my own. It had an intensity which at first I found hard to understand and it was, in fact, a long time before I realized that it was born out of contrasts. Later I began to appreciate those contrasts more and more myself, so that now when I think of Yorkshire and the Pennines it is to such places where the contrasts are seen at their most extreme that my thoughts turn. I am lucky, for I still have friends who live in the area, and every time I go back I feel a special lifting of the spirit. I love going back to what someone else once called this sweet and sour landscape.

Marsden is a typical mill village stuck at the very end of the Colne valley. To the east the valley widens out towards Huddersfield, to the west it is closed off by the steep rise of Standedge Fell. The town itself crouches down in that last hollow, its mills strung out along the thin ribbon of the Huddersfield Canal. Our friends live in a former lock cottage, and from the bedroom window you look out past the mill chimney, across the dog-tooth outline of weaving sheds towards the rim of the valley. People who have never known this sort of industrial landscape tend to think of it in terms of 'where there's muck there's brass', dour men and women eking out a poor living among the grimy terraces. The terraces are here all right, and the muck, but there's precious little brass these days – and there's certainly nothing dour about the people. And even if there is a certain greyness in the tight-clenched streets of the town, above and beyond them there is always the moor. Even in the bigger towns that moorland landscape of the Pennines is never too far away. You can look down the steep slope of a terraced row and see it waiting for you at the far end. And it is not mere fancy to say that town and country have a lot in common in these parts.

For me, lying in bed, early in the morning with the curtains pulled back, the view from the Marsden cottage can be superb. The valley rim has that hard edge where the Pennine spine sticks through the thin surface of the hill, forming a fine black line ruled between the green of the moors and the blue and white of the sky. The movement of the clouds up above and the movement of their shadows over the hillside keep the whole scene in perpetual motion. It is the sort of view that adds pounds to the bill at a four-star hotel. No one has ever built a four-star hotel in Marsden and I hope they never will. But it is hard to have to come to terms with the reality of life in Marsden. It was built on Yorkshire wool, an industry that comes to a halt here, for over the hill is Lancashire, where wool gives way to cotton. But what do you do with places such as this now that the textile industry is all but ended? Do you do as they have over the hill to the north in Hebden Bridge, where the mills now house craftsmen and artists? Do you prettify and gentrify the place? And if that solution does not appeal to you, what have you got left to offer instead to help keep the old place alive? There is no shortage of spirits here, no lack of guts, but there is a terrible shortage of jobs. It was in the Marsdens of this world that the wealth of Britain was created in the nineteenth century, but not much of the wealth stayed up here. And now that that is all over, there is not a lot of it coming back either. I just pray that it can survive, for there is a special character here of both people and place, a feeling that this town belongs absolutely within this landscape and no other. There is a sense of fitness that is sadly lacking in newer and fancier developments around the country.

People have always walked the hills here. In earlier times they were traders, leading long strings of packhorses across the hill tracks. Many now look back on this period as one where there was a better and a simpler way of life, and there have even been attempts to return to the old ways. One local family regularly travel by horse and cart and have even begun to use a packhorse. Good luck to them, but I fear they are living a delusion. Nostalgia is always selective in what it chooses to see when it looks backwards. Latterly the hills have been walked for pleasure. Locals have done so for years, but now it has all been made more formal and official. A couple of miles away the Pennine Way passes across Standedge Fell, and locals have now produced their own local route, the Colne Valley Circular Walk. We had intended to follow the route, but plans to follow the entire line were abandoned in the face of a 50-mile-an-hour wind that made progress westward decidedly slow. We settled for more modest ambitions. But if the gale-force wind made walking difficult, it did wonders for the sky, sending the big clouds rocketing past. It seemed a perfect day to be out and about.

We set out through the town and past the handsome Mechanics Institute. This is just being brought back into life as a theatre, cinema, community centre and anything else the locals can dream up to keep it going. Out of town, across the main road, and the moor begins; just a few minutes' walk was all that was needed to bring you out into the open. Right on the edge of the rough land stands the mill owner's house, foursquare and a little gaunt in the dark shades of the local stone. Up at the top is a turret room, an eyrie from which the owner had a choice of views: he could turn and look at the mill which had purchased the view, or he could look away up to the hills. There are no records to show which view was more favoured. I do know that I envy the owners that room. I told my wife that it would be my ideal study, but she pointed out, quite rightly, that in such a room I would never do a stroke of work; the world outside would prove far too compelling.

The hillside itself offers a familiar Pennine scene. Walls of dark gritstone mark the field boundaries, still in this part of the world dry-stone walls. No cement is used nor needed, for the wall is constructed by choosing the right stone for the right place. It is a craft which, thank heavens, is still alive. Yet these walls are more than just a pleasing addition to the land: for the history of the country can be found written in their carefully assembled stones. They could be used to pen in animals or mark off fields, but in either case they were marks of ownership – within these boundaries the fields are mine, within this pen the beasts are mine. From Saxon times when the valley floor was first divided right up to the great enclosures of the nineteenth century when the old open moorland was parcelled out, the walls have marked the changing pattern of ownership. Yet their most remarkable feature is not perhaps to be found in the chronicling of change but in continuity. The dry-stone wall has met the needs of generations of farmers and landowners largely because it is quite simply the best way of achieving an end: while ownership lasts, the walls will last. The wall of dressed stone and mortar might appear to be more stable but it will in fact suffer far more from the weather. Rain seeps into the chinks, nibbling away at the structure. In the dry-stone wall the elements flow freely – water runs away, the wind compresses the walls rather than demolishing them. So the walls recall the patterns of the years, seeming as much a part of the natural world as the rocky outcrops on the horizon.

If one looks down over the stone-built town, something of that same rightness can be felt. The town too belongs here; town and country do indeed have much in common. You can see this relationship most clearly in the hill farms, where the stone buildings sit just below the gristone edge which was their birthplace. Deep gulleys lead down from the edge towards the valley, and in a region that gets its fair share of rainfall these cloughs have proved ideal sites for reservoir construction. From Binn Moor above Marsden, the clough that leads down from Wessenden Head appears as a watery staircase of such reservoirs. Our route took us away from them on an easterly

Looking across Hebden Bridge towards Studley Pike.

path, parallel with the hill crest and with fine views across the valley. Down at the bottom, the mill chimneys poked up above the trees; above, the grey hill villages made patches on the land, while further up still the scattered farms and rising hills provided a mirror image of our own side of the valley.

Incongruously, a cobbled footpath appeared in the middle of the moor, overgrown and disused, passing on down between dry-stone walls. This was once one of the major packhorse routes of the valley, and following it down brought us to 'Nathan's', a terrace of cottages built in the middle of the eighteenth century. This was just the sort of community the packhorse route served, for you can see from the long windows on the upper floors that these were once both home and workshop to handloom weavers, houses where manufacturers worked before the first textile factory was ever built. Now they are derelict, sad empty places snuggling up to the steep curve of the hill. They represent a way of life that was finally ended by the factories on the valley floor, just as the factories too have become symbols of another age that has passed.

The route along the upper level of the valley is a fascinating mixture of the man-made and the natural. One farm, showing a prodigal use of stone, is reached via a raised causeway paved with thick slabs. The roofs on the farm outbuildings are covered in stone slabs as well, and one can only imagine the effort that had been required to get them up there in the first place. Away from the causeway, rough turf made a comfortable cushion for the feet, and everything seemed set for a good day's walking, except the weather. The clouds that were pounding in over Standedge were becoming steadily blacker and heavier and at last they fell apart under their weight of water. It was rain cum hail cum sleet and it did not exactly fall, but came at you horizontally. We scampered down the hillside to take the most direct route for home, the towpath beside the Huddersfield Canal.

We joined the canal at Slaithwaite – pronounced 'slough it' to rhyme with 'plough it' by the locals. It might seem difficult to incorporate such a completely artificial contrivance as a canal into an area of wild country, yet paradoxically canals often offer a wild corridor through an otherwise urban environment. Enclosed within boundary walls and hedges, creating their own linear world of water with rough footpath alongside, the canals have recently become as popular with walkers as they are with boaters. In the case of the Huddersfield, the walkers have it all to themselves, for the moment at any rate. It is derelict, but will not stay thus for ever, and restoration work is already well under way even if completion is still very far ahead. On this day the canal, navigable or not, qualified for the name wilderness in its own right. Winds whipped at the surface, the rain

Wessenden Moor above Marsden.

and hail stung our faces as head down we battled forwards. It had not been much of a walk in terms of miles covered, but it had supplied a rich mixture – sunshine and rain, open moor and historic buildings, mill town and country. It was the mixture that seems to typify the southern Pennines, but these southern Pennines formed only a part of my early hill-walking experience. For those who find the hillsides here too close to the other north-of-England world of mill and factory, then the northern Pennines offer something quite different to explore.

It was as a schoolboy that I first met and fell in love with the Three Peaks – Whernside, Pen-y-Ghent and Ingleborough. Our geography master was Mr Fairclough, a man for whom each generation invented the nickname 'Fairy', thinking it wonderfully original. Fairy loved the hills and was prepared to give up his weekends to take our unruly mob with him. If his primary aim was to teach us academic geography on our excursions, he failed: but if, as I now suspect, his main objective was to bring some of us to share his passion for the area, he succeeded. It was here that I learned to love the land and, just as importantly, was taught to respect it. I learned such necessary arts as map reading and the use of the compass, and something about personal limitations. I was to come back time and again, but more frequently with friends rather than as part of an organized expedition. I came back in all weathers and all seasons, and of all the seasons I liked the winter best.

Gritstone outcrops: the hard edge of the Pennines.

Each year, unhappily, one reads accounts of people setting out for the hills in winter and coming to grief. Some die, others are rescued, thanks to the efforts of a great many other people. In some cases the accidents are quite simply the result of misfortune, unpredictable and unavoidable; but in rather more the accidents were avoidable and occurred through ignorance. I mentioned earlier my own experience on Snowdon, when a change in weather turned an easy scramble into an excursion that developed an edge of genuine anxiety. This hazard is multiplied many times over in winter, when too many people return to wander the walks they had known in summer, and expect to be able to treat them in the same way in winter. Too often they are inadequately dressed, ill-equipped and have failed to take even the most elementary precautions to cope with the conditions – no extra clothing, no extra food and no means of signalling should anything go wrong. Consequently, if something does go even slightly wrong they find themselves in dire trouble. And the hills take the blame. Letters appear in the papers suggesting that the offending mountain should be closed off and people kept away. The correspondents generally turn out to have no connection with the hills or with hill walking, yet they usually justify their views by speaking up for the rescue party who would be the last people to endorse such views.

No one would dispute the need for proper care on the hills at any time, and most especially in winter. There might even be a case for a licensing system such as I found in the Canadian Rockies, where I had to satisfy the local rangers of my competence before being allowed onto the mountains. I would not go that far, but there is a lot to be said for another aspect of the Canadian system – the compulsory registration of routes together with the expected time of return. But no system can be made perfect, and it would be extremely difficult to monitor. Sensible walkers leave details of their routes anyway; the rest would probably not bother even if it were made compulsory. Many people seem to feel that such elaborate precautions are not needed anyway in Britain's comparatively mild climate and on the comparatively low hills. They can never have known what winter can mean on the hills – nor can they have known the misery of coming down from the heights with a lifeless bundle strapped to a stretcher. Only the inexperienced who have yet to learn and fools who will not learn treat winter walks lightly.

Having sounded that note of caution, we can now turn to a happier theme. Winter walks can be uniquely exhilarating, and the walks I have had on these hills in particular are among my happiest memories. Such walks are different in every sense from those of summer. For a start they need to be shorter. In summer it is no very great feat to walk all of the three peaks in a day – some even *run* them, but I have always regarded that as akin to madness. In the short days of winter when the snow is on the ground, one out of three can seem quite enough. With winter walks, however, there are certain other problems as well. On the one hand, the countryside can look so astonishingly beautiful that you could simply stand and look at it for hours. Unfortunately, if you do stand and stare for very long your feet get cold, and romantic views of the landscape seldom withstand for long the urgings of chilled toes. I always try to choose a walk that will be long enough to provide a sense of achievement yet short enough to be managed comfortably within daylight, with a certain amount of staring time built into the schedule. And there is one enormous advantage to visiting the area in winter. The 'beauty spots' that attract the summer crowds are peaceful again.

There are two beauty spots in particular which take on a totally different character when visited in the depths of winter, both within a few minutes' walk of Malham. It seemed a good idea to combine these with a one-way trip which was to be achieved by means of an early start and a judicious use of two cars to ensure one was there at the end of the route. There is a good general rule which says that the more elaborate the plan, the less likely it is to succeed. But occasionally, just occasionally, all the elements fit together to achieve something very close to perfection. We set out from Malham on a bright morning, the long shadows sweeping across snow as crisp as pork crackling. We were promised a fine day – and we had the world to ourselves.

Less than a mile's walk across the fields brings you to Gordale Beck, which can be followed upstream past a small waterfall, which gives a hint of the drama to come. The limestone that looks so pristine against the green of summer, now shows as shattered and knobbly yellow through the snow, but to balance that the ground which can be churned to mud by visitors is pure white. But the best is still to come, for you walk round a scree slope, turn a corner and there it is, Gordale Scar. I have often wished that news of such a place could be kept a secret – no accounts written, no photographs shown – but it is much too late for that, and here I am adding my twopenny-worth. But how wonderful it would be just to come upon it, knowing little or nothing of what to expect. An eighteenth-century traveller described his sensations in a sentence bristling with astonished capitals:

'Good Heavens! What was my Astonishment! – The Alps, The Pyrenees, Loch Lomond, or any other Wonder of the Kind at no time exhibit such a Chasm.'

Though we can no longer experience that delightful, fresh shock of discovery, winter provides an opportunity for rediscovery. The gorge is always dramatic, a cataract hurtling down between beetling walls, but a harsh winter transforms it. The roar of the falls is replaced by an icy calm. The rushing waters become a confection, frozen icing dripping over the rocks. Winter also provided easier access to the deeper recesses of the gorge. The whole place has become in any case more accessible in recent years, since the authorities have provided a wooden staircase for visitors – an addition which is by no means universally welcome and certainly does precious little to help preserve the sense of wild beauty that has always marked the Scar. However, in winter you can take a more direct route, free of the spray that would give a summer soaking. A rock ridge leads up beside the fall to the point where the last remaining un-iced trickle pours out through a window in the limestone. A winter visit is now the closest you can hope to get to the open-mouthed amazement of the eighteenth-century traveller.

The exploration of Gordale Scar complete, another short walk leads across to the next of the Pennine wonders, Malham Cove. It is, if anything, even more spectacular than Gordale Scar, a crescent of crags, some 300 feet high and overhanging the base a full 14 feet. At the base a stream gurgles up which is to become the River Aire, eventually to wander off to the industrial heartland of Yorkshire at Leeds. No hint of that appears here, where the effects only call to mind phrases such as 'majestic, magnificent, awe-inspiring', cliché words which, for once, can be justified for they are no less than

Gordale Scar.

accurate reflections of the effect of the scene. It does have a regal grandeur, and it does inspire awe at the thought of the natural forces that have carved away the land to produce this spectacle. But this is only a part of the Malham story. You can ascend to the top of the cove – and again the authorities have seen fit to provide a staircase for the purpose, though in winter it is more hindrance than help. You could, of course, always emulate the local rock climbers instead, who with the aid of bolts and drills have engineered their way up the cliff itself.

Reaching the top, you find the third and in some ways the strangest of the sights of the area, the limestone pavement. It reaches to the very lip of the cove, a landscape of stone blocks, divided one from the other by deep grooves. It is a purely natural phenomenon. Rainwater, containing carbon dioxide in solution, eats into the limestone. The fine cracks become the weak points where future attacks are concentrated until with time the whole plateau reaches its present condition, divided up into blocks like the old road setts. Technically, it is known as a karst plateau, the blocks of which are clints and the cracks in between grykes – lovely hard words for a hard limestone world. Even without the labels attached, the pavement remains a dramatic exemplar of the power of natural forces to shape and change the land.

Having reached this point, you could simply declare that duty has been done. The most exciting and dramatic features of the region have been duly visited, noted and enthused over and a good deal of energy has already been expended in clambering up and down, so that the siren call of opening time could be answered with a clear conscience. But these are only the Pennine highlights, and the portrait would be hopelessly incomplete without the subtler tones that are introduced with more intimate knowledge. The way onwards lay towards Malham Tarn and takes us back to the Pennine Way again, which seems to keep popping up all the time, wherever you walk in the North of England. If you are not coming across the main route, you are stumbling over one of the alternatives, for if the Way does not offer all things to all men, it does offer alternatives between hard going and easy. But in winter there are few indications to suggest any way at all. The smooth whiteness spreads all around, covering footpaths and tracks. In summer this is a well-trodden way, much used by students from the local field centre, but now the marks have been obliterated by fresh snow, just as our own tracks would soon also disappear. The tarn itself is not much of a place, a wide expanse of water set in a landscape which is surprisingly flat for this part of the world. Now, at least, it was shimmering brightly, where the ice crept outwards from the margins to glint in the pale sun. They say Charles Kingsley dreamed up the idea for *The Water Babies* here, but if so it is not easy to see what gave him the inspiration. Perhaps if the scenery had been more exciting he would have been too much preoccupied to sit around thinking of plots for books.

Far more exciting for me was the prospect of the open land up ahead, the steady swell of Fountains Fell. Names can still tell us a lot about the land. There are quite clearly no fountains in this part of the world, but the name does remind one of another famous and much frequented beauty-spot, Fountains Abbey. Within the old ruins you can conjure up images of the ascetic monks contemplating the magnificence of the creation, while alternately chastising themselves for their sins and praising God for the riches of the world. So it was, at first, but as time went on the riches of the world became ever more important in the life of the abbey. The monasteries became wealthy, and Fountains was as rich as any. The Abbey is some 25 miles away from the fell, but the land here was acquired as part of the grazing for the thousands of sheep that were the principal source of wealth. Sheep still graze here, if not at this time of the year, but the abbey has long since been no more than a picturesque ruin.

Fountains Fell is not one of the great peaks but rather a prelude to the greater bulk of Pen-y-Ghent rising up ahead. But in the snow, the distances seem to stretch. The afternoon sun gains a little strength and the firm snow begins to soften. But as feet sink that little bit deeper, making the effort to lift them just a little greater, so the prospect ahead becomes ever more enticing. Pen-y-Ghent offers a summit to aim for, a vantage point from which to view the world, and its own skyline promises some dramatic scenery. You need to keep those enticements in mind, for the short drop down from Fountains Fell leads to a far steeper climb up ahead. Here the snow conditions proved a definite advantage, having reached just the right consistency. On a steep slope, hard snow can prove too slippery, so that you have to kick steps up the slope; soft snow lets you sink in – half-way in between and it provides just the right amount of give. It is still comparatively hard work, just enough to produce a comfortable, warm glow to counteract the touch of ice on the gentle breeze. Add to that a pale blue sky, edging down through ever paler shadings until at the horizon it blended in with the white of the snow and you have the perfect conditions for a winter walk.

The summit of Pen-y-Ghent is ringed by limestone, but topped by darker gritstone which stands out in sharp relief. But elsewhere the summit rocks were softened by the sinuous lines of cornices curling outward over the lip of rock. It was like a land newly made, so perfect that it seemed indecent to disturb its purity. Nevertheless, we carried on upwards towards the crags which look rather more imposing as you come up towards the base to find the easiest and safest route to the top. It is by no means a difficult ascent, but it is infinitely rewarding as

you stand on the summit cairn looking out across the open land to Ingleborough. Coming down, which should be easier than going up but seldom is, can be especially trying in the snow. You can descend quickly. I once came down this same hill by glissading, which is like ski-less skiing, using an ice axe as a brake. I very nearly broke my neck. Since then I have come the cautious way, digging in hard to be sure of a footing. Fortunately the way here is made easier by the presence of the wall leading down from the cairn.

The angle eases and the land becomes an affair of lumps and hollows. The lumps often turn out to be the snowed-up mounds of shooting butts and some at least of the hollows contain the other great features of the limestone belt, pot-holes. Hull Pot is the most spectacular, a gaping wound in the land which is alternately filled in wet weather and emptied in dry. Many of these pots are regularly explored by teams of cavers, but it needed only one day's slithering around in the underground dark to convince me that this was a pastime I was happy to leave to others. Yet, oddly enough, if someone told me that this was a man-made shaft, I would be off down it like a ferret after rabbits. I find it absolutely fascinating to explore the world that man has created for himself beneath the earth, but have never been that keen to explore the similar world created by natural forces. So the pots remain holes in the ground to me, to be peered into and then left severely alone.

The afternoon sun seemed to be dipping quite visibly as we headed for the narrow lane that led on to the road into Horton. The toy car at the lane end grew into a genuine vehicle usable by grown adults whose legs were getting weary. There was a marked quickening of the pace at the thought that only a short journey now separated us from a warm fire and a pint of Yates and Jackson. I was even prepared to swallow local pride and swallow Lancashire ale with it. Sitting back relaxing and talking over a thoroughly satisfying day, it was hard to recall that much of the ground we had trodden would in just a few weeks' time be full of people, and the now empty roads between the piled-up snow banks would be crowded with cars. But even if I could have emptied the hills for a day's solitary summer walking, I would not have exchanged that for the day just gone.

Bronte Land:
the moors above Haworth.

10. The Lake District

The Pennine hills have a special place in my memories, for it was there that I first took up serious hill walking. The Lake District has a similar hold on the affections, as the district where I went to start what was to become even more of an obsession, rock climbing. It was not, strictly speaking, the beginning, for I had served an apprenticeship on the gritstone outcrops of Yorkshire, at Ilkley and Almscliffe. There you can find technically difficult routes, but they are all short. You climb up the crag, walk back down and get ready to start up again. It is excellent training, good climbing, but somehow not quite the real thing. For that you need the extra height on the cliffs that turns the climb into a much more extended exercise, a steady progress towards a distant goal and, just as importantly, incorporates the climb into the mountain world. The slog up the fell is as much a part of the whole enterprise as the rock climb itself, and the mountain scenery has a vital role to play. For rock climbing for me has always been more than a matter of gymnastics. Indeed, the great majority of climbers I have met have seen the sport as a way of bringing them into a closer, more intimate relationship with the hills. And in moving from small outcrops to extended climbs, you are doing far more than just extending the length of the route. Other factors, such as weather, take on a new significance. The challenge is no longer purely technical, but involves the climber in a full range of understanding of the hills.

This book is not really intended as a series of personal reminiscences of a long-lost youth, but the stories keep appearing simply because present-day responses to the countryside are a result of all that has gone before and, in many ways, draw on first impressions. I was fortunate in that, living in the north of England, the mountains were easily accessible, and it was perfectly possible to dash up to the Lakes on a Friday evening, spend the weekend climbing, and dash home again – possible but not easy. Some of my contemporaries were already at work and could afford such luxuries as motorbikes – no one in our lot ever rose to the luxury of a car – but I was still a sixth-former. I had no money, so if I wanted to get to the hills I had to travel by rule of thumb, joining a long procession lined up on the Skipton to Kendal road, each distinguished by a coiled rope threaded through rucksack straps. I always enjoyed hitch-hiking. Some I know disapprove of the activity, but no one is forced to give a lift and I know that in more recent years, as a motorist myself, I have always been glad of the company on a long journey. In the course of a hitch-hiking career that took me from one end of Britain to the other, I met many interesting people and took many interesting journeys. But none could ever compare with that first visit to the Lakes.

I had arranged to meet my climbing companion in the bus station at Skipton and I found him waiting wearing a smile that indicated

Lake District crags above Hard Knott Pass.

pleasure and a certain smug self-satisfaction. Not only had he managed to get a lift from Bradford, but the driver had volunteered to hang on and wait for me to take us both on the next leg. This was excellent news, but the big surprise was still to come – the vehicle was a magnificent, shiny Rolls-Royce. No wonder Pete looked smug. We were extraordinarily fortunate, not least because our driver was an enthusiastic amateur geologist, and as we creamed along through Clapham and Ingleton we were given the benefit of his knowledge on the limestone escarpments which we had walked so often without really understanding anything of the underlying structure of the hills. Journey's end as far as the Rolls was concerned was Windermere. From there we could see across the lake to the Langdale Pikes, and it was one of those moments that require no camera to record them, for it is far clearer in memory than any photograph could ever be. A red sun was setting behind the hills, stippling the wavelets on the lake. The hills themselves stood out like two-dimensional stage settings. There was an air of unreality, for the shapes were so precise that they seemed to have been cut out from a book of Lakeland views and then enlarged.

The gentle hills around Windermere.

Yet the clarity which should have made them seem more real served only to increase the sense of theatrical magic.

More mundane thoughts soon intruded. We caught a bus to the lake end at Ambleside, and there motorized transport ended. But if there were no more buses, at least the little stall which in those days did the world's best cheese and onion sandwiches was still open. Fortified, we set out on the 7-mile walk to Langdale. Walking on through the dusk the hills steadily grew in front of us, their looming presence quite dominating the silent road. Past Elterwater and Chapel Stile we went and on into the heart of the Langdale valley towards the lights of the two hotels, the New and the Old Dungeon Ghyll. The latter marked, and still marks, the end of the valley road. It would have spoiled the perfect introduction to the area if the pub had been closed, but fortune was still with us and there was a pint to reward our labours. Coming out, we took to the road again which now swung away towards the south and the tortuous back road that returns to Amblesdie via Little Langdale. Just where the road crosses the stream there stands an old stone farm building, Wall End Barn, which to my generation was a home from home. It did not offer much in the way of comfort. You simply went in and slung your sleeping bag down on the floor – but it was dry and kept warm by the fug from the number of bodies it contained each and every weekend. And all this came for the princely sum of one shilling per night – and no chance of getting out of the payment for Caleb, the local farmer, was round at dawn, clattering his change and demanding is broad Cumbrian accents, 'Shekels gentlemen please. Shekels.'

This was my introduction to Lakeland. The next day we climbed one of the simplest routes in the area, Middlefell Buttress – simple, but with 250 feet of rock face it was by far the longest route we had either of us tackled, and however easy it might have been we were both puffed with pride. Over the next few years, I became a regular visitor to Wall End, spent many an evening at the Old D.G. as it was universally known, and moved on to climbs a good deal more demanding than Middlefell Buttress. That was to become more or less a short cut, a quick way of getting up the fell to save a long walk to Gimmer Crag. Then I left the north, settled in London, married, pursued a career and did all those things you are supposed to do at that age – and somehow those things did not include visiting Great Langdale. And when I acknowledged that climbing was out, for I had been away too long ever to get back to the old standard, and turned instead to walking, I still kept away. Langdale was climbing, and I was no longer a climber. It was also, in my time in the fifties, a place that was still comparatively free from tourists. Motorcars were not so widespread as they are today, and the M6 had not then arrived to

bring the world and his wife quickly and easily to the Lake District. I *Little Langdale.*
still visited other parts of the area, but never Langdale. I simply could
not bear the notion that it might have changed out of all recognition.
The old haunts would have gone and the wonderfully vivid memories
would be warped by a new visit. It was only in the 1980s, when I set
out on the series of walks for this book and I was already beginning to
indulge in a certain nostalgia, that I decided to risk it. For so long the
Lake District had meant so much to me, and most of what it meant
was tied up in this one valley. It was time to return.

There was no way in which the trip was going to be an action replay
of my youth. No hitch-hiking for me this time: I drove my own car
and I felt quite disappointed at not being able to repay old debts, for
no one stood by the roadside waiting for a lift. Driving the last part of
the route from Ambleside in the dark, it seemed much further than I
had remembered, and I wondered what had happened to the young
man who thought nothing of doing that walk with a full rucksack on
his back. I certainly thought very little of the notion now. I had hoped

to stay in the Old D.G. – Wall End barn was definitely in the past – but the hotel bedrooms were closed for redecoration. So my wife and I settled for the New, and a very fine, old-fashioned, comfortable sort of place it is too. One thing I had been careful to avoid during this exercise in nostalgia was crowds. We had chosen the last weekend in November, and when we sat down to dinner we had the place to ourselves.

It seemed slightly 'wrong' to be staying in such circumstances. I had never stayed at either of the Langdale hotels before, and had never even had a beer in the New – which was considered 'posh'. Yet here I was being served with food instead of pumping up a primus, and going up to sleep on a bed instead of a pile of straw. I felt positively guilty. But that silliness vanished the next morning. When you sit down in the morning, lace up your boots and set off for the hills, the true essential nature of the place asserts itself.

That morning we left the New Dungeon Ghyll Hotel, rather later than we had intended, noticing for the first time that the name 'New' derived from the fact that it was built as recently as the 1860s, the date being spelt out in stones at the doorstep. The forecast was for good weather, but the clouds were squatting down on the tops, so that only the lower slopes were visible. We set off down the road between neatly railed-off fields, already occupied by sheep brought down to the winter pasture. These are long-haired sheep, their fleeces all but dragging in the dirt, so that they might seem little more than perambulating doormats were it not for the magnificence of the heads peering out above the woolly blankets. Sheep are, in popular mythology, stupid animals, but they have bright, alert gazes – handsome in their own way. They are trying to live down their bad press, and they baad a welcome as we made our way to the point where road gives way to track, though I could not resist the impulse to deviate from the intended route to call in at Wall End. Alas, it had changed. Where I had slept, calves munched and the days of Caleb the Shekel Man were clearly ended. So I returned to the track that led up the valley.

Even though the clouds still clung to the hilltops, the nature of the valley itself was plain, a giant scoop eaten away by the glaciers of the distant Ice Age. The floor is flat, and the hillside rises steeply all around. But though the pattern was clear, it was frustrating not to be able to see the full extent of the Langdales, not to have a glimpse of the Pikes rising up above the fell. Even the lower slopes had clinging wraiths of dense mist, a glum picture that bore no resemblance to the bright promises of the cheery radio met. man. It was by no means an unfamiliar experience to be walking along the rough, rock-strewn valley floor, while looking for a view that was quite obscured by cloud.

Buttermere.

Yet there was something odd about the scene. Peering up at the grey clouds I could see what appeared to be a flock of giant birds hovering above the hills. But what sort of bird was so big, or could remain so still in the air? It was a mystery which temporarily remained without a solution, for the mist closed up the gap again, tumbling down the hill, to obliterate my dark flock.

It is an eerie experience to walk along such a cloud-topped valley. Every now and then the mists part to give tantalizing glimpses of the uplands and then close in again. Ahead and to the left, the path rose up towards Bowfell which I remembered as a wild track, scarcely discernible among the rocky slopes. But such is the current popularity of the area that my insignificant track has now become a major highway for walkers. Known as The Band, the path has steadily eroded as more and more walkers use it, fanning out from the original line, as increasing wear makes it muddier and more difficult to follow. I had thought, at first, to follow that route, for it too was a reminder of earlier times when three of us had tackled the high pass in winter, hacking a way up with ice axes. Now, however, it simply looked dark and grim under its grey canopy, so we struck off along the more inviting, northern side of the valley.

One difference soon became apparent from the days when I had first come this way: walkers were now being channelled along defined paths, a necessary measure to prevent excessive wear to the land. It seems incredible that the tough granite of the area should ever wear away, but the ceaseless pounding of heavy boots does have a very pronounced effect. If these measures suggest a desire to dictate to walkers, to confine them to neat and tidy made-up paths, then I am happy to relate that this is by no means the case. The ways may be regulated, but they are still rough and ready. The ground is stony and crossed by a multitude of little streams, coursing down from the still shrouded hills. The streams meet to form Langdale Beck in the centre of the valley floor, and as the end of the valley grew nearer so the converging streams all met in a flat, green expanse of spongy grass which gave a splendid springiness, very welcome after the stony way. At the same time as we reached the grassy heart of the valley, the clouds began to fragment, and my flock of giant birds was revealed for what it was. What I had taken as dark patches against the light sky were rocks poking through the snow that had already dusted the uplands. It came as a surprise, not because snow at this time of the year was unexpected, but because in the warped perspectives of the mist and cloud, the marks had seemed far too high above me still to be a part of the land. It was splendid now to have at least a glimpse of the heights that lay ahead.

The end of the valley represents decision time. If things look really

Grasmere.

bad, you can turn round and head for home. Alternatively, you can head up via any one of a number of routes towards the valley rim. We opted for Stake Pass, the easiest of the ascents, for it seemed a sensible compromise in the still uncertain conditions. That matters were genuinely uncertain was confirmed when we saw a second party approaching: one man clearly well in the lead, the rest spread out behind. As they got nearer, the shrill whistles from the group made it plain that these were no hikers, visiting the land for recreation and pleasure. They were shepherds, working men whose lives were spent on the hills. It was the oldest of the group who joined us first, two lolling-tongued collies at his heels already panting and tail-wagging in anticipation of a little excitement. The shepherd, pink-faced beneath a fine flat hat of violent check, stopped to chat. The main subject of conversation was, as seems always to be the case with anyone connected with farming, the weather. Would the cloud break? Would it stay fine? Would it, in short, be possible to round up the hill sheep and bring them down to safe grazing in the valley? It could have been no more than a wish to seem polite to ask the opinion of someone who would never gain a fraction of the experience of Lakeland weather that he clearly possessed. But there was rather more to it than that: he wanted reassurance. It was difficult to gauge the shepherd's age: his smooth, cherubic face showed little sign of wear, but I would have put him in his sixties. He was concerned that the year was drawing on but his helpers, younger but, he suggested, if only obliquely, less dedicated than himself, were reluctant to venture out in dubious weather. An earlier excursion had proved abortive, for the howling wind had drowned out the men's whistles to the dogs. Yet he felt that other days had gone by when a group of determined workers could have done the job, but the determination had been lacking. Hill farming is a business that cannot succeed without dedication. The financial rewards are low, but other rewards can be immense – immense, that is, for those who cherish this way of life. The old shepherd neither knew nor wanted to know anything else, but he looked upon himself as one of the last of a line of such men who had been happy in the hills, regardless of material fortune. The young men ambled along, some distance behind, when we set off for Stake Pass and the promise of better weather.

We left the lush greenery of the valley for a route that followed a narrow, busy stream. I tried not to huff and puff too noisily as the shepherd, many years my senior, strode smoothly on. I might have been short of breath, but I was at least happy to find the short, springy turf under foot, providing an ideal walking surface. And for that I was grateful to the man ahead of me, hurrying to his sheep. For it is the steady munching of the sheep, up and down every hillside, that keeps the land as we see it today. Without their busy jaws, the grass would be far longer and the going a good deal more difficult. So I panted on, feeling the pull in calf and thigh, watching the mist break and re-form around me.

Then, quite suddenly it seemed, the world changed. The pallid grass was lost beneath a thin layer of crystalline snow, while simultaneously I climbed up above the grey cloud and into bright sunlight. The valley remained a grey sea, but now the peaks came up as islands and even as I watched the cloud broke into tattered flags that waved briefly in surrender and vanished, leaving the world spread out below me. Such moments cannot be planned, but when they come they make all the day's efforts worth while.

We lingered over the view, which seemed pure enchantment. The Lake poets who knew this land and knew such moments sang its praises. Unwittingly, perhaps, they encouraged many to rush to see what they had enjoyed in solitude, and often it seems that the crowd can never obtain more than a glimpse of the genius of the place. The old problem recurs yet again – how to share the wonders of the wilderness without destroying the wilderness in the process. On this day the problem seemed to evaporate with the clouds: it seemed far less grave than it sometimes appears. Those who hunt out the magic will find it; those who do no more then step out of their cars and wait for the magic to be revealed may achieve some pleasure, but will never come to any true understanding of the land.

We had been promised a fine day, and now the promise was being fulfilled. In the distance we could see a second party of walkers on the broad and broadening path of The Band, heading towards Bowfell. Beneath us the valley was spread like a cloth threaded by the bright silver ribbon of the stream heading out towards the distant waters of Windermere. On either side of the valley the screes fanned out beneath the crags, the remnants of thousands of years of weathering of the rocks. These are not the most spectacular scree slopes in the Lakes by a long way: that honour belongs without question to those of

Receding prospects: the hills of lakeland.

Wastwater, steep and menacing, reaching down to the water's edge. Yet these gentler slopes have their own fascination. Looking across the gully I could see the screes of Pike of Stickle, a name with irresistible fishy associations: the graceful, rocky hump of the mountain does indeed have a look of the spiney stickleback. But there is more to the place than that, for what we were looking at were the remains of a factory, though one that has been out of use for a few thousand years now. This was a neolithic axe factory where stones were shaped to form axe heads and the evidence is still there among the debris of the scree where you can hunt for part-formed axes and flakes lopped off in the process. You need a keen eye to find and recognize them, but they are there all right.

The shepherd had no time for such reflective pauses and was already on his way and over the top of the pass. We followed on, heads down to watch for footholds on the rough ground beneath the layer of slithery snow. For a time all I saw was the ground beneath my feet, and all I heard was the rhythmic pounding of blood in my ears. Then the way eased, and we came up over the valley rim to be faced with the welcoming sight of a wide expanse of moorland, speckled white and brown as the taller bunched grasses poked through the thin snow. If you have staggered on this far simply to get a good view, then you get your due reward. In the distance Windermere gleams, far more impressive from here than when seen from the crowded road that runs along the eastern shore. And all around are the other Lakeland hills, ready and waiting for exploration. Up at the head of Borrowdale are some of the finest of the peaks – Great Gable and Scafell, England's highest mountain. But we had more modest ambitions, a simple tour of the Langdale Pikes round to Stickle Tarn and then back down to the valley. The days were too short for major expeditions, and though everything was now sunshine and brightness, I had no wish to be caught up here when dusk fell and the temperature plummeted. A timely reminder that the hills should indeed be taken seriously came with the arrival overhead of the Mountain Rescue helicopter. It also came to mind that they were enjoying the same superb view, but had achieved it with a lot less effort. Admittedly they had not come to admire the view and, even if they had, they had more than earned their rights to it. I would certainly never refuse the chance of a chopper ride over the district but I still hold to the opinion that nothing ever gives the same satisfaction as a view that has been earned. It is not just the puritan ethic that says you should work for your pleasures: it is also the fact that the actual business of walking brings you into an intimate relationship with the land which gives extra meaning to the distant prospect.

The walk across the moorland at the top of the Pikes is invigorating without being demanding, across an undulating plateau from which the hump of Harrison Stickle rises up. Beyond the smooth shoulder of the hill lies Stickle Tarn, one of those splendid places that make the effort of walking seem worth while. It is really quite a small pond by Lakeland standards, but in its wild setting beneath the bulk of Pavey Ark, where the granite crags were spotted and streaked with the snow that topped ledges and filled crevices, it possessed true grandeur. And there is no way that anyone can enjoy the scene, apart from the helicopter men, who has not made a real effort to get here.

From here we eventually took the steeper but by far the more spectacular route down, along the deep gully of Dungeon Ghyll. At this height it is only a mild indentation, but soon it begins to slice deeper into the fell and the pathway degenerates into a bare slope of sliding stones. Inevitably the route always looks easier on the opposite side, and equally inevitably if you go to the trouble of jumping from stone to stone across the bubbling water, you find you were deluded. So we resisted the temptation and stayed on the western bank, scrabbling down beside the vigorous stream. There was now no sense of urgency: the sun had some way to go before it dipped below the horizon, so there was plenty of time to stop, select a comfortable rock seat and enjoy the view of the gorge with its tumbling waters and cascades. Below, we could see the other aspect of the life of Langdale. Here were fenced and walled fields instead of open moor, and the tiny dots of grazing sheep. We were not alone. An owl swung lazily out across the hill face and headed down to the valley, making an early start on the night shift. But otherwise it seemed a place of solitude and even the noise of the valley life was lost beneath the rumble of the waterfall. But the day would not last for ever. The sun dropped below the valley end, throwing its last brightness over the hills. It was time to complete the last stage along the well-worn track beside the ghyll to the hotel at the foot. It was only later when thinking about the sudden change in the sky and the brilliance of the evening colours that I began to experience that odd sensation of *déjà vu*. I could not recall seeing just such a sunset in just that place, yet it was undeniably familiar. It took a while to identify the feeling, but it came to me in the end. I had not seen it – I had read it. It was that greatest of all recorders of the Lakeland scene, William Wordsworth, who had sat on such a hillside and watched the sun above the lake.

> Already had the sun,
> Sinking with less than ordinary state,
> Attain'd his western bound; but rays of light –
> Now suddenly diverging from the orb,
> Retired behind the mountain tops or veil'd
> By the dense air – shot upwards to the crown

Of the blue firmament – aloft – and wide;
And multitudes of little floating clouds,
Pierced through their thin ethereal mould, ere we,
Who saw, of change were conscious, had become
Vivid as fire – clouds separately poised,
Innumerable multitude of forms
Scatter'd through half the circle of the sky;
And giving back and shedding each on each,
With prodigal communion, the bright hues
Which form the unapparent fount of glory
They had imbibed, and ceased not to receive.

It had been, in every sense, a splendid day: my fears had proved quite unfounded. Whether I should have felt quite the same if I had come in high summer is quite a different matter, but on this day at least, my first impressions had been confirmed. The Langdales were just as I had remembered them. True, there were minor differences, such as the paths on the lower slopes that were now clearly defined, but none of the essential character had been lost. There was, however, still one last test to be made. The Old Dungeon Ghyll had always been the great meeting-place, where we would spend the whole evening talking over the climbs of the day, while eking out in slow sips the few drinks a meagre budget could afford. I have often wondered how Sid Cross, the owner, ever put up with us, for we were really most shockingly bad customers. But then Sid was a mountain man himself, and at least he knew that whatever money did get spent by us in Langdale went over his bar counter. It was always a rough and ready sort of place, with sensible stone-flagged floors that had borne the tread of generations of heavy-booted climbers and walkers. Now, if only that had all remained the same, then I felt that my faith in mankind was justified. And, miracle of miracles, it had. The beer was still, mercifully, real beer and the talk was still of walks and climbs. If I felt like the Old Man of the Hills with my reminiscences of days gone by, then that was only to be expected. It was of no importance, what really mattered to me was that the Lakeland fells held the same appeal as ever – and that same appeal is being felt and appreciated all over again by another generation. It was a comfortable thought on which to end the day.

Wrynose Pass: a typical
glacial valley spread out
below the hills.

11. THE HIGHLANDS

Doom-ridden Glencoe.

The northern end of Loch Lomond from Inversnaid.

Where do you begin to discuss the mountains of Scotland? My first thoughts turned towards Skye and the Cuillin Hills. I have spent three summers in Skye, enjoying climbing on the best rock in Britain, gabbro, a rock so rough that it practically removes your finger prints but provides wonderful holds for feet and hands. In fact the climbing is so good that one is even prepared to endure the worst horror that Scotland can perpetrate – the Skye midge. This is a vicious little beast and practically unstoppable, simply regarding any insect repellant with which you might choose to besmear your person as a tasty aperitif. But, on reflection, I decided that the walker could never get the best out of Skye. It offers the finest long hill route in Britain in the traverse of the Cuillin Hills, but it is limited to those with some expertise in rock climbing. For the rest, it can offer frustrations.

What then of Britain's highest mountain, Ben Nevis? The highest peak it might be, but it is also unfortunately one of the dullest. To climb it in summer is simply to engage in one long slog of a walk which offers much perspiration but little inspiration: to climb it in winter is to move away from the mountain walk and to enter the world of mountaineering. Alternatively, you might wish to turn to Scotland's famous winter sports centre, the Cairngorms, but the growing popularity of the ski centre has had a pronounced visual effect on the landscape. This can be seen at its worst at Aviemore where the

hills compete for attention with a grey, ugly block of a building. To describe it as inappropriate for the surroundings is to take understatement to the limits. It is a visual offence, a crime against the scenery.

One answer is to look towards the less popular areas, towards the names that are not bandied about with the frequency of Ben Nevis or the Cairngorms. How about, for example, paying a visit to the Cobbler? It is not by any means the highest peak in Scotland, for it stops short of the 3,000-ft mark, but as the ascent can start at sea-level, you might have every single one of those feet to climb. In fact, when I went up there I even started below sea-level. I had arrived at Arrochar at the head of Loch Long in style, travelling on a Clyde Puffer, one of the last of these fine old steamers which for generations carried the cargo of the Scottish west coast. Our ship, *VIC 32*, had been adapted to take a dozen passengers, and after spending a day stretching my arms in shovelling coal into the boiler, it seemed it was time to stretch my legs over the hills.

We were moored up at the eastern end of the loch, when I came up from my cabin below the waterline, adding those few extra feet to the climb. A group of us set off round the head of the loch to the point where a mountain stream plunges down through the forest and the mountain track leads upwards. Soon the trees were left behind and we came out onto the open moor with the rocky peaks of the Cobbler itself sticking up in imitation of the cobbler's last that gives the mountain its name. As you climb, so the view opens out and a most extraordinary sight met my eyes, like a hallucination or a mirage. Our little steamer was far below on the sea loch, but now another steamer appeared far to the west, a steamer that seemed to hang in the air just below the top of the distant hills. The explanation was soon obvious. I was seeing Loch Lomond and its resident steamer, *The Maid of the Loch*. The reason it seemed so bizarre was that I was still thinking of water level as the tidal level of the salt-water loch, not at all the same level as that of the inland lake. The mystery was solved – which was rather a shame really. It would have been pleasant to have been able to boast of having seen a ghostly ship above the highlands.

The summit of the Cobbler, when you finally get there, is very fine, with sheer rock faces rising out of the steep slopes. Two climbers were out on what looked a most interesting route, very steep, but with neat, clean holds, just the sort of climb that offers a degree of airy excitement without being too impossibly difficult. I watched for a while before taking my own tame route up to the saddle which separates the twin peaks, paid my respect to each prominence and then took a rest to watch the world around me. It had been a thoroughly pleasant walk on a fine summer's day, yet there is something undeniably irritating about walking all that way with quite a

Glen Shiel.

steep route up to the summit only to find a shorter, more gentle route leading to the same spot from the other side. Not that I would have wished to take the alternative route, but because it was there it somehow reduced the sense of achievement which is part of the pleasure of getting to the top of a hill in the first place. It is not the only reason, but it is a reason, and it had been diminished. Next day we chugged off again round the sea lochs and islands, while the steam whistle echoed round the hills to announce our departure. It was enjoyable, but somehow there was an element missing, a lack of some essential ingredient that proclaimed that this was the Scottish Highlands, and could be nowhere else in the world. It was some time before I could isolate that basic ingredient, but I got there in the end: it was a sense of history.

The history of the Scottish Highlands has not, in recent times – and by that I mean the last three centuries – been a happy one. Certain places now have a brooding melancholy which seems to epitomize the tragic past. Perhaps that is mere fancy, for the land would after all look much the same whether the local inhabitants had died happily in their beds or come to some horrible, blood-bespattered end. But we cannot divorce our knowledge of our place in the land from our feelings towards the land. There are certain places where the past hangs in the atmosphere as real and tangible as the morning mist, felt on the senses as keenly as the smell of blossom after rain. I went to an area where two aspects of the past seem to me to have just that quality – the first shows the face of tragedy, the second is more difficult to define, for it contains elements of comedy and farce, foolishness certainly, but also a kind of heroism.

Glencoe is a deep mountain pass which at its eastern end opens out on to the vastness of Rannoch Moor. I have never visited the pass without thinking of the massacre of 1692. It is an event that holds a special dishonourable place in the annals of infamy, an event from which neither English nor Scots emerge with very much credit. Everyone, it seems, has heard of the Glencoe massacre, and most know it involved the MacDonalds and the Campbells, but beyond that many are a little vague, unsure even which were the perpetrators and which the victims. Perhaps the story is best forgotten, for it is a tale with few redeeming features, but as it acts so strongly upon the imagination of visitors to Glencoe, it is as well to set down the old narrative again.

Jacobite resistance to the rule of William and Mary was broken at Killiecrankie, and the Highland chieftains were required to swear their allegiance and that of their clans by the first of January 1692. There was much reluctance and several put it off until the last moment, and among those was MacDonald of Glencoe. The old chieftain at last set out in vile weather to ride to Fort William but the officer in charge declared himself unauthorized to accept the oath and sent him on again to Sir Colin Campbell at Inverary. Campbell was away from home and, when he returned, refused to take the oath on the grounds that the last date had now passed. MacDonald, an elderly man, pleaded his case, arguing that the winter roads had delayed him and, at last, Campbell agreed to administer the oath. MacDonald went home content. The treachery had begun.

The oath of loyalty had been taken late: on that all are agreed – but it was accepted, or so it seemed. No doubt that would have been the end of the story had there not been bad blood between the Campbells and MacDonalds. The MacDonalds, on their return from Killiecrankie, had raided the Campbells' cattle and this action had served to fuel the discord between the pro-English and Jacobite factions. At the end of January a troop of soldiers of the Earl of Argyll's regiment under Captain Campbell marched into Glencoe, but assured the worried inhabitants that they meant no harm and only needed billets for a while. So the troops were quartered, spread among the families of Glencoe. In mid-February Captain Campbell received his orders – the clan was to be put to death. The pass was to be closed so that 'the old fox, nor none of his cubbs may gett away'. The government, the letter declared, did not wish to be 'troubled with prisoners'.

At five o'clock in the morning the signal was given and the massacre began. Thirty-eight were simply hacked down or shot, but the sheer enormity of the act saved many more. The Campbell soldiers were Highlanders like the MacDonalds, had enjoyed their hospitality, and now had little stomach for this grim business. Families escaped, but to be turned out of your bed and sent out on to the winter hills in night clothes is as sure a death sentence as a sword in the belly. For every one who died at the hands of a soldier, two perished in the cold on the high passes. Those who made it out of Glencoe faced a second hostile reception in the next valley. The settlements in Glencoe and in the side valley of Gleann-leac-na-muidhe were destroyed and the life went out of the glen. It might seem that life has now returned in good measure as cars scurry up and down the main road through the pass, while walkers and climbers swarm over the surrounding hills. But the true life has gone, the community has been destroyed. Those of us who come here now are mainly temporary visitors, a constantly changing population. And that as much as anything gives the pass its eerie, haunted atmosphere – and if anyone wants to argue that the atmosphere is not a reality but a reflection of dim memories, then so be it. No objective measure can be applied to decide how much of Glencoe's unique atmosphere exists as a physical reality among the rocks and heather and how much arrives in the visitor's head.

The special character of Glencoe can be felt even by those who do no more than drive through, particularly as is so often the case in the Western Highlands when the clouds sit lowering on the peaks. Then the pass becomes a dark, gloomy tunnel. The hills rise steeply on either hand while the clouds form the roof. To be out in the open on such a day should reinforce the effect, yet paradoxically it seems not to do so. Certainly the atmosphere is felt, but not with that glowering unfriendliness that can assail the driver. There seems to be something peculiarly nasty about being enclosed in a high-speed metal box in such an environment. In other places it is probably a great comfort not to feel the wind and rain, to be insulated from the weather, but the forces in Glencoe can seem so malevolent that your box appears to be a very insubstantial shell indeed. If I were ever to see the ghost of a murdered MacDonald I would expect to see it peering at me through a rain-washed windscreen. Your box not only protects you from the rain – it protects you from reality as well.

Those on foot have no such problems. I have often stood on a hillside looking down at the narrow pass and imagined that distant day, but the doom-ridden feeling does not linger. It is at its strongest when you see the pass as a distant prospect. Close to, rain, wind and cloud become no more than the familiar accompaniments to a walk in the hills. Rain makes you wet, the wind pushes against you and the

Loch, moor and mountains, all the elements of Highland scenery come together in Glen Shiel.

clouds mask landmarks that should be your guides. They are physical difficulties to be overcome, not mystic phenomena. There is nothing like the need to find your way over a wild, wet hillside to concentrate your mind on the present. The hills here are characterized by their high rock faces, split by deep gullies which offer routes to the summits only a little less demanding than those faced by the rock climber. To the north the view is dominated by the crags of Aonach Eagach, to the south by the Three Sisters, while at the eastern end is the most impressive of all these hills, Buachaille Etive Mor. It is no easy task to reach the rocky summits, but it is possible to penetrate to the heart of the hills. The simplest method is to take the pathway that runs along the stream, Allt Lairig Eilde, cutting right through to join the River Etive on the far side of the hills.

Those who want to take a high-level route must learn patience, for it is possible to stay here for days on end and never see the tops emerge from under the clouds. Such was my fate last time I came to Glencoe, when I had to be content with walks on the dripping lower slopes. But I do have memories of happier visits, and those memories at least tell me that if you spend a week in waiting and get clear weather at the end, then the wait will have been worth while.

The River Coe which runs down the centre of the glen, fed by a multitude of hill streams, once provided the dominant theme for the valley. For centuries, the only roads were the drove roads, but to these were added the military roads, first begun under the direction of General Wade. They were not built to serve the local population, but to keep them in order – and even if they had been intended for the locals they would have been of little use to them. The native Highlanders had long since found their own favourite routes through the region, and the military roads followed quite different lines. They started with a disadvantage, for survey parties were most decidedly not welcome in the hills. Instead, lines were drawn on the map with military precision, and squads of soldiers were sent out to do the work. They had little experience of road surveying and construction techniques and they were led by officers with less. Routes were pushed along the valley floor until they could be pushed no further, at which point the hill was attacked through a series of violent zigzags. They were, however, the first modern roads in the region in the sense that they were built on decent foundations and provided with adequate .drains. Along these roads the soldiery daily marched, while the life of the region flowed around them along very different paths. In more recent times the main trunk road was built alongside the river and has now become the most obvious feature on the valley floor. To the walker, the river and its tributaries continue to be of major importance, since their crossing-points determine the starting-points

for walks, and the gullies cut by the streams provide the gaps in the rock defences by which walkers can reach the summits.

I had a fine day's walking starting at the Study, a rocky knoll beside the main road, and apart from the fact that it provides one with a simple way to climb up a little above the valley to study the land, the name was for a long time a mystery to me. Then I heard that the Gaelic name for the hillock is *Inneoin*, meaning an anvil, which given the shape of the rise is quite appropriate. Then the word 'study' turned out to be an old Scots dialect name for an anvil. So, once you work your way back through the old language and half-forgotten names, the whole thing finally makes sense. From here you can follow the river westwards as it cascades over falls and tumultuous streams hurl themslves down the hill to swell its waters. Just beyond the most spectacular of such spots, the Meeting of Three Waters, a name which requires no gloss, the first of the corries is met which lead up to the summit of the Three Sisters. But for those who are prepared for a stiffish climb, the second corrie offers a superb route up the mountain. It follows another stream in a deep gully hemmed in by craggy sides, which end only at the rough hillside leading to a small plateau beneath

An all too typical view of Glencoe from Rannoch Moor.

the rocky peak of Stob Coire nan Lochan. Here the ground is decidedly soggy, but a number of choices are on offer – along the sharp ridge of Gearr Aonach, for example, or a gentle meander round to the summit of Aonach Dubh. If you take the latter route, you can see on the rocky flank the entrance to Ossian's Cave. A busy man, Ossian, much given to house moving, for he seems, if local stories are believed, to have occupied every cave in Scotland. And for those prepared for another climb over rough rocky terrain the ridge can be followed to the south providing an alternative route to the top of Stob Coire nan Lochan, 3,657 feet above sea-level. Having reached that point you can truthfully say that you are looking out over some of the finest scenery the Highlands can offer. And anyone who is not moved by the splendour of Glencoe spread out all around should perhaps consider giving up hill walking altogether.

The hills will always be my first love, but they do not represent the whole story or even the whole of Highland scenery. Away to the east is the birthplace of the River Coe among a multitude of streams and lakes on Rannoch Moor. My first introduction to the moor came many years ago when I crossed it from south to north with no difficulty at all, travelling not on foot or by car but by railway on the old West

Glencoe:
the haunted valley.

Highland Line. And this brings in my second slice of history, a story with all the elements from farce to near tragedy, but one which puts our own efforts into perspective. For the men who set out the railway in the nineteenth century took a walk across the moor which I would certainly never have attempted.

Many things have to be done before you can begin to build a railway, including looking over the ground and deciding where to put it. The West Highland Line from Glasgow to Fort William had to cross the moor and so a party set out to explore the route. That all sounds very reasonable until you look at the party, the time of year they chose for their expedition and the arrangements that they made. The party consisted of three engineers, Forman, Bullock and Harrison, Robert McAlpine, the contractor, McKenzie, a Fort William solicitor, and two factors from local estates, Martin and Bett. John Bett was then sixty years old, and of the whole group only one man, James Bullock, had so much as set foot on the moor before. And this motley crowd were planning to make a 40-mile journey in the dead of winter setting off from Spean Bridge on 30 January 1889. A certain amount of planning had gone into the operation, but as good Scots all, they should perhaps have paid heed to the words of the national poet on the subject of 'the best laid schemes'. Messages were sent that were destined never to arrive, appointments made that were not to be kept and guides sent for who would never appear. Things began to go wrong from the very first.

On the morning the coach dropped them at Inverlair Lodge, and from there a guide was to take them 2½ miles to the tip of Loch Treig. The first planning failure was now recorded – no guide was in sight. So off they set, dressed rather more for a day in the city than a walk through the wilds of Scotland. Two of the party, conscious perhaps that the weather might prove inclement, carried umbrellas. The first stage of the journey safely accomplished, they were to proceed by boat down the lock, but predictably neither boat nor boatman could be found. When both were finally located, they set off in the fading light of the afternoon in a leaky boat which had to be frequently bailed out with boots. Rain and sleet hurtled at them out of the gloom, and it must have been with a sense of immense relief that they eventually reached shore and were met by two gamekeepers who were able to lead them to Lord Abinger's hunting-lodge. Here they were supposed to have been met by a hot meal and comfortable beds, but by now they would have been less than astonished to find that the messenger with the instructions had failed to appear. A scratch meal and a huddled night under thin blankets was all the comfort they found. The next day was to prove far worse.

They set off early on a morning dark with heavy cloud and with little abatement in the sleet that still whipped across the loch. A climb took them to the edge of the trackless desolation of Rannoch Moor. Their destination lay 23 miles ahead. They had no guide, were inadequately equipped, one of the party was elderly and the weather was foul and showed no signs of improvement. Yet on they went, brave but hopelessly foolhardy. Anyone who has ever set foot on Rannoch Moor will know just what they found, a great morass broken by tufts of wiry grass. Your choice is to move with difficulty from tuft to tuft or sink deep into the mud: either way progress is slow and difficult. They set off for yet another arranged meeting, this time with Sir Robert Menzies who was to have walked out from Rannoch Lodge to discuss the line. He, sensible man, stayed at home and sent his gamekeeper instead to invite them back to the lodge for the night. Incredibly, with nightfall only a few hours away and another 15 miles of bog and moor in front of them, they declined the offer and squelched on. Of all the absurdities perpetrated on this journey, this was the greatest folly of them all. The consequences were inevitable.

Old John Bett was the first to succumb to exhaustion as they staggered on into the dusk, soon to be followed by McKenzie. Bett could go no further and Martin and Harrison stayed to tend to him, providing what comfort they could. At last a use was found for the umbrellas which were made into a makeshift tent. McKenzie carried on a little further but then he had to stop with Forman. That left McAlpine who had not the least idea where he was or where he should be going but who set off anyway on his own to look for help. Bullock, who had at least been on the moor before, thought he knew where he could locate a cottage and he too wandered off into the night, where he succeeded only in finding a fence. Unfortunately, he encountered it before he saw it, fell, knocked himself out and remained unconscious for hours. When he came to, he had at least enough sense left to realize that a fence signified habitation. He followed it to a track and the track led at last to two shepherds who set off at once to find the miserable party still out on the moor. They reached them long after midnight by which time the old man was only semi-conscious and had to be carried to a nearby hut.

The following morning the journey was at last completed, though there was still no sign of McAlpine. But that robust individual had found his own way to safety after marching alone through the long night on the moor. All were safe and no great harm done. But it was a desperately close thing, just how close became clear the next day when a blizzard brought heavy snow to blanket the moor. Had it come sooner, it is doubtful if any would have survived. So those who travel the line today should look out of the carriage window as the train takes its lonely route across the moor to Rannoch Station and remember the men who came this way when there was no railway, nor indeed track of any kind.

The coming of the railway has inevitably brought its own changes to the land, but if you leave Rannoch Station, arriving by train or road, and walk out onto the moor, you will have some notion of the sort of terrain the railway pioneers met a century ago. An even clearer impression can be obtained by approaching from a quite different direction, starting from the mountain rescue post at Kingshouse Hotel just off the main road from Glencoe. A good track leads off towards the Black Corries Lodge, a comfortable walk of some three miles. Beyond the lodge the way divides, the main route continuing straight on, while a second track leads off in a more northerly direction. The main track then begins to zigzag on through a morass very like the one the travellers had struggled through in the dark. You can keep your feet dry by staying on the route towards Loch Laidon, but stray just a few yards from the path and every step becomes a struggle. It is hard work in daylight, but in the black of a winter's night country like this leads only to nightmares. A multitude of streams cross the moor, pools and lochans dot the ground.

Having reached Loch Laidon you can turn north where the rising ground of the Black Corries offers drier footing. The highest point of these hills reaches less than 2,500 feet, but from the top you can look out over the wide expanse of Rannoch. Streams pour down every flank of the hill to mingle, diverge and meet again in the bog below. And there to the north, beyond Blackwater Reservoir, is the line of the railway. From the top of the hill a gently sloping ridge leads down to a little knoll and the second track that will keep you clear of the worst of the bog. How easy it all seems with good maps, compass, fine weather and a decent track: how different if deprived of these benefits. Perhaps it is no more than the memory of such near-fatal expeditions as that of the railwaymen that gives the moor its slightly sinister air. It makes you wary, and wariness is no bad thing. This is a true wilderness. It is not dramatic, in the way that Glencoe is dramatic and I must confess I have never felt it to be other than alien and inhospitable. Yet there is also a great sense of spaciousness here, a spreading to far horizons and even an eerie beauty. If I look rather wistfully towards the hills to the west, there are others who find a unique fascination in the moor. It is unique, but I cannot in all honesty say that I find it a great pleasure to walk. In fact, I am still half inclined to prefer the train. I am grateful to Mr McAlpine and his companions, but I am quite sure I would not have wished to join them.

12. Cape Wrath

It is all too easy to categorize Scotland, dividing it up into cliché-labelled compartments. Here is The Monarch of The Glen, here Yon Bonnie Banks and Yon Bonnie Braes and over there The Tartan in The Heather. But there is so much more to enjoy than is implied by the labels. There is also in the far north-west corner a region which combines elements which elsewhere in Britain tend to be kept in quite distinct categories; for it combines a mountain landscape as wild as any in the country with a coastline far wilder than the rest. It was this combination that drew me to the furthest tip of Scotland, known as Cape Wrath. The name itself is the first attraction, with its promises of huge seas, great winds and a melodramatic combination of the wildest cliffs and the roughest weather. Such is the power of words, even misunderstood words, on the imagination. For the name has no such connotations of divine fury, but is simply an adaptation of the Norse name 'Hvarf', meaning turning-point. This is where you reach the corner of Scotland and can look out over a grey sea to a limitless horizon, for now no land lies between you and the polar icecap.

We came to the area by car after having enjoyed a brief visit to Orkney – too brief as it turned out, for this group of islands has a unique fascination, and I can think of few places where I have felt so content. And not all the contentment can be attributed to the effects of Highland Park, the deliciously smooth malt whisky distilled on Orkney. It was a mixture of place and people and atmosphere which made the leaving sad and the determination to return absolutely firm. In places, notably on Hoy, the islands are as wild as one could wish, but it is not the sense of wildness that calls so powerfully. Here I felt was a community which was aware of its place in the continuum of history, and the ancient history of the islands is your constant companion wherever you go. But if the islands themselves do not feature in this narrative, they did provide the perfect prelude to what was to come. Above all, they slowed us down. My wife and I came to Orkney burdened with the normal share of twentieth-century *angst* – the Orkneys wiped it away. By the time we left to return to the mainland, we had slowed down to a good, respectable and thoroughly civilized pace. When we drove off the ferry at Scrabster we were relaxed and at ease – which was perhaps just as well since the roads we were to follow were never designed for people in a tearing hurry.

No doubt there are those who suffer agonies of frustration as they drive along the north coast of Scotland. They dream of zooming along a motorway at speed, instead of which they are faced with a nominal A road which is single track throughout most of its length and which wriggles and jigs around hills and sea inlets defying you to go fast. And why should you want to speed? Perhaps we were lucky, arriving at the tail end of summer, but it was one of the few occasions in recent years

The ferry to Cape Wrath crossing the Kyle of Durness.

when I actually enjoyed driving a motor car. Traffic was, to say the least, light and it seemed that whenever another driver appeared in the distance, we would both pull in to passing places, indicating polite priority to the other. 'After you Cecil: no, after you Claude.' The country was wild but the behaviour civilized, a most happy reversal of the norms of motoring.

Cape Wrath was the area we intended to explore, and the Cape Wrath Hotel the base for our operations. Getting to the hotel seemed in itself to be part of an adventure, for the country was so desolate, so uninhabited that you were given the distinct impression that if the car ever broke down you might never get away again. Durness, on the edge of the Cape Wrath peninsula, soon dispels any such notions, for it has been touched now by the finger of tourism. The café and the gift shop have arrived, but have not yet dominated the scene. And Durness provides an interesting lesson in how different generations with different ideas have changed and adapted the bits and pieces left behind by their predecessors. Representatives of the armed forces came here, set up camp, a typically ugly conglomeration of concrete huts, and went away again leaving their detritus behind them. So what do you do with these all-but indestructible lumps on the land? The local answer has been to develop a craft centre. This sounds very fine, but names like craft centre can cover a multitude of strange activities

The Kyle of Tongue, on the north coast of Sutherland.

and are all too often applied to the manufacturers of fancy knick-knacks. This is not so here where in surroundings that seem to be designed to destroy any image of true craft and beauty, a motley array of weavers, potters, candlemakers, stained glass designers, leather workers and many more have contrived to produce something of real worth and value. And these are no summer visitors, no gaudy butterflies settling for a brief period before returning to warmer, more comfortable climes. It is a year-round community that is working hard and making Durness their home. And bless them too for having the best café for miles around – real home baking and not a plastic plate or frozen pea in sight. Not that we had that much need of extra sustenance for the Cape Wrath Hotel is not an establishment that is going to let its guests starve.

Some locals might perhaps regard the craft workers of Durness as foreign invaders of this corner of Scotland, but they seemed to me to be far more involved in the life of the region than the seasonal invaders – the English visitors, myself among them. We are now the major industry of the region, and a great many people make a living out of looking after us. Some, like the Cape Wrath Hotel, have been at it for a long time. Their main objective in life is to cater to the needs of those hoping to pluck salmon from the local rivers or pelt the feathered population with buckshot. We, it soon appeared, were the

The lonely landscape of Cape Wrath.

only visitors whose sole objective was to enjoy the scenery. That became obvious as soon as we stepped through the front door. Inside the hall was a table like a fishmonger's slab laid out with the day's catch, each fish labelled with its weight and the name of the fisherman. A book inside recorded still more details of the how, the when and the where of the removal of these Moby Dicks of the salmon world. None it appeared had come from the waters owned by the hotel, but had been plucked instead from the privately owned reaches some miles away. Later we were to meet the owners.

They gathered before dinner, and soon the air was full of esoteric conversation, and full is the only word you could use. The males were not merely dominant, but domineering in the way that only the English upper class can be. The women were strictly divided. Those who fished barked an accompaniment to the male chorus; the rest knitted. Seeing them come in earlier, they were a drab lot, dressed in sensible out-of-doors clothes designed purely and simply to keep the elements at bay during the day's fishing at the distant salmon streams. But come the evening and the fishermen came into their own. The women remained somewhat dowdy in soft tweeds but the men were far more extravagant: garments of a loudness that would have brought a blush to the cheeks of a self-respecting bookmaker, suits of plus fours which if worn on the hills would have sent the game scampering for cover. Their conversation was out of Evelyn Waugh, their clothes from P. G. Wodehouse – Bertie Wooster on a day when he had neglected Jeeves's advice.

They seemed to me to be absurd. A gentleman plonked himself in front of the fire, plus-foured legs spread, hands stuck deep into jacket pockets, and gave forth political views somewhere to the right of Genghis Khan. Because I found such attitudes repugnant, I wanted to think of them as crass outsiders, bursting in on this wonderful, wild country I could see through the hotel windows. So in a sense they were, but in another sense they were true countrymen. For all their outward pomposities, you cannot get away from the fact that each of these big, red-faced men had tramped 5 miles over rough moorland, stood all day either beside or in a cold, fast-flowing mountain stream, straining to catch each nuance of movement in the water, and then marched 5 miles back again. They had in their own way an encyclopaedic knowledge of this particular, distant stream, an awareness of every natural feature that affected their prey, the salmon. I shall never be at home with these people, never share their attitudes, but I cannot help but respect their awareness and knowledge of the country.

The Cape Wrath peninsula has one supreme advantage over other wild areas of Britain – you cannot get a motorcar anywhere near it.

But, because life is rarely perfect, it suffers from a balancing disadvantage which sadly it shares with too many other such places. Being beautiful and remote it is considered an ideal spot for the military, in this case the Navy, to lob in shells. A glance at the map shows the ferry crossing the Kyle of Durness, but the track on the other side is covered in the ominous red lettering, spelling out DANGER AREA. So, although cars cannot reach the area, to get to the Cape you need to take the ferry and then the minibus, the one vehicle that has been shipped across. Once at the Cape, however, you are on your own and can make your own arrangements to be collected.

The ferry itself is quite an experience, not because the trip is especially exciting but because the ferryman is such a splendid character. We first met him in the evening when we had strolled down to the shore. He had moored his little motorboat and repaired to the hotel for a dram and as all devotees of the malt will acknowledge, to take just one dram is an insult to a decent whisky. Tides, however, pay heed neither to man nor dram and by the time the ferryman was ready to depart, he found his boat high and dry. We volunteered our assistance and were rewarded for our endeavours by a non-stop and colourful commentary on the ways of tides and boats which lasted until we had eventually got the vessel back into its rightful domain. We waved him off into the dusk as he bobbed across to the distant shore, having left us with the promise of a free trip the following day.

It is somewhat frustrating to be faced by splendid country and then be forbidden to walk through it, but Cape Wrath itself is the great compensation. This is not really walking territory at all – though the energetic, prepared to camp along the way, can reach here from the south – rather it is a great natural phenomenon, a place of stark grandeur. The cliffs of Cléit Dhubh rise 850 feet above the waves, the tallest in Britain. They are not just high but sheer, a giant vertical wall of rock. This is the scenery that makes this far corner of Scotland unique. Near the Cape the sea has eaten through a projection to form a natural arch while the stack rises up from the water with its horizontal strata so distinct that it looks like a crazy pile of giant plates. The Cape itself has the one sign of human life, the lighthouse 370 feet above sea-level.

The Cape is a grand place, wonderful to visit, but it is only one magnificent feature in an altogether magnificent area. Away from the tip of the Cape there are any number of attractions for the walker in the unique mixture of mountain and moorland, tall cliffs and almost equally impressive dunes. There are walks in plenty in every direction and you can simply choose whichever suits your mood of the moment. Take a step off the single-track road in any direction and the wilderness at once engulfs you. Turn this way and the glen leads down

to Loch Dionard under the graceful 3,000-ft peaks of Foinaven, haunt of the rare ptarmigan. This bird of the high moorland is a protected species, and the locals are careful to preserve it. But there are always one or two self-styled 'sportsmen' who set out to shoot the ptarmigan. If they are caught, and there are still a remarkably large number of keen eyes and ears in this lonely region, they will find their day's shooting comes expensive. The last one to be nabbed had to pay a £300 fine.

The walk to Foinaven was one of the treats we had promised ourselves, having heard of the magnificent views from the summit when on a clear day you can see to the Western Isles. Loch Dionard itself, ringed by cliffs, was an extra attraction. But as we stepped outside to join the fishermen eyeing the weather it was plain that there would be no view of the Western Isles that day. 'Not too bright', remarked one, a master of understatement, for the clouds reached almost down to the loch. It seemed a good day to explore coast rather than hills. The coast offers, in fact, a rare treat for it is very seldom in Britain that you get the chance to walk across beaches, over dunes and along clifftops in complete solitude. That is just what the area can offer. We took a route round the eastern shore of the Kyle of Durness, down to Faraid Head, then back through Durness to Smoo Cave. The weather was, indeed, not too bright. It was remarkably wild but just the sort of weather you want to bring a touch of drama to a walk by the sea.

Beinn Spionnaidh, rising above the head of the Kyle of Durness.

There is no path as such round the Kyle. You simply choose whatever line you fancy and set off. You soon leave behind all signs of habitation but you are not short of company. The whole place is alive with rabbits. Everywhere you look you can see them – sitting twitching at the entrances to burrows, munching peacefully at the spiky grass and then, as you come into view, presenting you with the sight of a rapidly disappearing white scut. And the sky above is no less busy, and not just with the expected gulls. Ringed plovers can be seen, and even a raven came down from the nearby hills to poke around a bit on the lower levels. Most charming of all are the dunlin, little brownish birds showing white on the wings and tail, that turn up regularly to give aerobatic displays in formation. They zoom past at low level, climb up from the water in a smooth curve in line-ahead formation and then swoop down again in a spectacular dive with many a change of direction along the way. The dunlins' miniature Farnborough is a constant delight and the coastal scenery is no less so. As you come round the first headland you get your first glimpse of Balnakeil Bay, a superb expanse of white sand, overlooked by the ruins of a little seventeenth-century church. It is astonishing to find any beach at once so clean, so beautiful and so deserted. We meandered across the sand and took the path through the high dunes to Faraid Head. The peninsula is a mere 2 miles long and less than a mile across at its widest point yet it offers an extraordinary visual mixture. The tall dunes, their tops whipped into gritty plumes by the wind, dominate the western side, while rocky cliffs fall down on the east. In between, the ground underfoot varies from coarse grass and heather to shifting sand.

Our ultimate destination lay beyond Durness – Smoo Cave, a natural phenomenon as well known locally as the cliffs of Cape Wrath. It lies at the foot of a deep cleft and you can see how the cave was formed if you cross the road at the top of that cleft. A stream draining down from Loch Meadaidh suddenly vanishes to cascade down through a hole to a point far below which marks the beginning of the cave system. There is no access at this point, but a steep path leads down the gulley to sea-level and the dark vault. Inside, the waterfall is still a distant splash, for this turns out to be only the outermost cave of a complex system. You can see the inner cave by crossing back over the stream, Allt Smoo, and clambering up to a ledge to peer down into it, and still the 80-ft-high fall remains a distant object of admiration. Further exploration of the Smoo system demands the equipment and expertise of the pot-holer. But even the casual visitor can get a genuine thrill out of the descent of the steep path to the 50-ft-high arch of Smoo Cave.

Having tasted, as it were, the parochial delights of the coast round

Durness, we decided that the time had come for an exploration of the peninsula by an approach from the south. Our first objective was Sandwood Bay. We drove round to Loch Inchard and then along the loch side to Oldshore More, where the peat track led away to the north. It was the sort of day where you hoped for the best – but prepared for the worst. Overhead, the sky was a brilliant blue but a southwesterly gale was sending cloud racing out from the sea. With luck they would keep racing on, otherwise we were in for a thorough downpour. We set off across a field where the long grass was flattened by the wind. Heather sprang out of a black peat bog, which is used in a small way for fuel. In some parts of Scotland peat cutting has become big business, but here it was more like the peat cutting I had known in Ireland, where the local farmers took no more than they needed for their own fires. This was much the same – a few piles of cut peat by the track with a wheelbarrow for transport as the nearest thing to mechanization in a system that has changed little over the centuries.

The well-defined path winds between a string of small lochs fed by brown peaty streams. A mile from the road and you feel that you have already reached close to the heart of the country and the local wildlife seem to take little interest in the intruders. Two fat grouse waddled solemnly and imperturbably up the path like pompous frock-coated Victorian bankers. Unhurriedly, they took note of our approach and wandered off into the heather where they were lost from view. We tramped on watching the clouds blow up, occasionally giving us the benefit of their contents but soon blowing on again leaving the wind to dry us as fast as the rain had dampened us.

At the end of the last of the small lochs, the path climbed up a low ridge from the top of which a splendid prospect opens up in front of you: Sandwood Loch, a wide expanse of windwhipped water and beside it the ruins of a croft. It seems an amazingly remote spot, so many miles from other habitation, and you would need to have a real love for the lonely beauty to want to live and work here. The land is still used – sheep run everywhere, over the moors and up the tall dunes that still form the last barrier between us and the sea. It is possible perhaps to look at the sheep and think that things have not changed that much after all. But they have. The next day I was talking to the old gentleman who was working the petrol pumps near Durness, and as we chatted about the area I mentioned the walk to Sandwood. He certainly knew the place, for he had been born in that small house by the loch and in those days it had formed part of an estate managed from Kinlochbervie Lodge, now a hotel. It was well farmed and was also a sporting estate, Sandwood Loch being a famous salmon water. Even that has changed, the sand has encroached across the land, blocking the gulleys that lead to the sea. Part of the life of the region has died, but from neglect, not from wilful vandalism masquerading under the name of good commercial management as happened throughout this region in the last century.

To the south is the vast tract of the Reay Forest, though there are few enough trees to be seen here, just a landscape of tiny hills where every hollow contains its small lochan. Traditionally, this was the land of the Clan MacKay, but in 1829 it was bought up by George Leveson-Gower who set about evicting thousands of families, destroying the crofts to make way for sheep. It was just one episode in the tragic history of the Highland Clearances, which sent tens of thousands not merely from their homes but from their native land as well. When we walk these empty hills enjoying the grandeur of the scenery we should occasionally pause to remember that we are walking over the graveyard of the Highland way of life. It was destroyed so that a few could profit from sheep – or so that fewer still could march out to shoot the grouse and the deer. There is little now, perhaps, to be gained by speculating over what might have been. Crofting is all but dead on the mainland, and there is little chance of its ever returning. But you cannot help feeling with the old man at the petrol pumps that when a house such as that at Sandwood Bay crumbles, something in the life of the region dies as well.

I have to be honest and say that none of this occurred to me until

Across the sea to Orkney.

that chance conversation. At the time I was simply entranced by the whole scene and was soon to find even better things ahead. The path runs above the loch, round the flank of a low hill, Druim na Buainn, to the high dunes covered in tough, spiky marram grass. They rear up above the land, sculpted and shaped by the wind to an extraordinary purity of form. No footmarks scarred the smooth surface or disrupted the elegant curves. The dunes have an abstract beauty that might have been shaped by a Hepworth or a Moore. And there, beyond them, lay the bay itself – a mile of flat, white sand edged by the crashing rollers of the Atlantic. Not another soul was in sight, not a Man Friday had left a footprint in the sand. The sole inhabitants seemed at first to be the wheeling seabirds but as we came nearer to the shoreline we could see the inquisitive black snout of a solitary seal poking out above the waves. It watched us destroy the unblemished smoothness as our boots sank into the sand. I have never I think been to a finer stretch of coastline, for it even rivalled my beloved beaches of Cornwall and certainly I had never been to such a place and found it deserted. And then to complete the scene, the thin drizzle eased, the sun shone out and the two combined to form a perfect rainbow over the sea.

Away from the beach, the coastal scenery is just as magnificent. At both ends of the bay the land begins to rise. To the north the cliffs lead on in almost unbroken procession towards the tip of Cape Wrath. To the south, the scenery is equally spectacular. We clambered round beneath the craggy face of Druim na Buainn to look down towards the tall detached rock stack of Am Buachaille. Then, at last, we turned back towards our original path. The day had given us not merely magnificent scenery, but scenery topped by magnificent skies. Now, however, those skies were darkening in a decidedly ominous manner. The weather timed its onslaught to perfection, waiting until we had reached the heart of the peat moor, where there is not so much as a shrub to offer shelter. Hail and rain swept straight into our faces, and there was simply nothing to be done but put your head down and keep going. It is at the end of a long, cold, wet tramp like that that one of the great secrets of Scottish life is revealed to you. You discover why whisky was ever made in the first place, for surely no one has ever found a better solace than the malt. And to take a dram of one of the Islay malts in particular, with its strong aroma of peat, is not just to be warmed and comforted but to be taken back in the mind to the best of a wonderful day.

Soon we had to pack the car and head for home but we grabbed what we could of the country along the way. We followed the minor road round the coast on its roller-coaster course. You climb hills so steep that the view in front is only of sky, then pop over the top to dive down a slalom course on the other side. It is almost enough to reconcile you to the fact that you are back in the mechanized twentieth century – almost but not quite. Here are even more tracts of tempting country, yet to be explored, waiting for another day. Here are superb mountains, the daunting sandstone bastions of Stac Pollaidh and the most impressive, the shapeliest and most dramatic of all Britain's hills – Suilven. It is always sad to leave such magnificent mountain scenery, but as we stopped on the roadside at the top of a small hill and stared out towards Suilven at least we could sit and plan the next walk and the next expedition. It had been my first visit to this north-west corner of Scotland but I hope it will not be my last. Of all the places I had visited, not just in the course of preparing material for this book, but in years of walking and climbing, this seemed to me to have everything that I wanted: not just mountains and moorlands, but a coastline that was still wild and not home to a thousand cara-van parks.

So we drove on southwards past places which were far more familiar, to Inverness and along the Great Glen to Fort William. It was not long since I had last come down this way, not walking but working nevertheless, shovelling coal in that splendid old steamer the Clyde Puffer. Fort William does little to hold the attention, a town bestrewn with souvenir shops that has lost all sense of identity. It is one of those centres where people stop who are 'doing the Highlands'. It is a centre which epitomizes the dilemma that recurred time after time throughout my travels: can you provide unlimited access to the wild places yet keep them wild? If the answer is 'yes' then there is no problem – but if the answer is 'no' then the problem is there and mighty intractable. Keep areas free of motorcars, don't allow in the coaches – make people get on their two legs and walk if they want to enjoy the country. Concessions can be made for the sick, the elderly and so on, but let the rest make an effort. It is an attractive argument, seen from my point of view. But for every one of me, there are a lot of others who quite simply want to look at the mountains without walking. Have I any right to deny them the pleasure? The argument was presented even more forcibly as we drove down south to join the nose-to-tail traffic that even out of season creeps along the side of Loch Lomond. One solution for the individual, even the car-bound individual, is to use a little initiative and find another way, which in our case meant the far more attractive road along Loch Long. But that is not really the answer. So at the end I suppose I have to declare myself and settle for one point of view.

Some places are now so popular – Snowdon, Loch Lomond, Malham, Dovedale – that there seems little to be gained by trying to keep the crowds away. They create problems, notably erosion, but that has to be tackled pragmatically, with efforts being made to control movement to keep some sort of conservation policy at work. This means limiting the freedom of individuals to come and go quite as they please, but otherwise access must be total. There are other areas, such as the Peak District, where experiments are being tried out whereby there is limited car access, but a kind of minibus service to take non-walkers into the hearts of the valleys, and that seems an altogether adequate compromise. But there are other areas where, I believe, all attempts at providing better access for vehicles should be met with total resistance, where the inroads of agriculture should be kept within the strictest limits – in short, there are areas which should be kept wild. And it is no use marking off a pocket-handkerchief patch of ground and labelling it a country park in the pretence that you have kept a true piece of wilderness intact. And for those who would argue that this is élitist, I would put this case. Even if those who want to push a road through the middle of some remote Highland glen outnumber the rest of us by ten to one, the right lies with us. For we are speaking not just for ourselves, but for generations to come. They have no voices yet, but if the wilderness is destroyed now they will never get the chance to put forward an opinion. The natural beauties of our wild places can so easily be destroyed and once destroyed may never be regained. In these crowded islands of ours they offer thousands a chance of freedom and an opportunity to experience the deepest of pleasures. Such views might be termed élitist, but at least they are not élitist in the more usual British sense of being tied to social class. In fact, one of the factors I have always found most appealing is that there are no social barriers among those who come to the hills – my first companions in climbing were a public schoolboy and an apprentice plumber. And I would in fact deny the charge of élitism completely, unless an élite is defined as a group who take more than the common measure of delight in their surroundings. I believe that more than ever we need the wilderness for it reminds man, the most wilfully destructive creature on this planet, that there are still places on the edge of civilization which can make him aware not of his strength but of his weakness. Man can smash atoms, travel in space, hold an arsenal of weapons that can demolish half the solar system, but once let individual man stand in the middle of the open moorland as the storm clouds gather and he becomes no more than another small scared animal. The wilderness can teach us about beauty and strength, but if it can also teach us a little humility then long may the wilderness remain.

Having declared that this is not intended as a guide book to specifically recommended walks, it might seem somewhat perverse to provide details of those walks. Nevertheless, there may be readers who will find the following information of value: those who do not, have a simple remedy. They may, at this point, lay the book to one side and go out walking. Those who read on will find indications of access to the different regions, a notion of how to follow the various routes, should they wish to do so, and a short list of books that are specially valuable as guides to those regions. The appropriate Ordnance Survey (OS) 1:50,000 maps are indicated for each area and where they exist the 1:25,000 Outdoor Leisure Maps (OLM). More precise locations are given National Grid references.

Anyone attempting to follow any of these routes should remember they do so entirely at their own risk and should take all sensible precautions to avoid getting into trouble. It is the individual's right and privilege in this country to walk freely over much of the land, and even to risk an accident, but those who treat the matter lightly should bear in mind that they are frequently forcing others in subsequent rescue parties to risk their lives as well. So please take the obvious precautions when walking in open country. Always check on local weather forecasts, and whatever the forecast may say, take adequate supplies of waterproof clothing. Take a map and compass, but remember that these are of little use unless you understand how to use them correctly. Take food, a torch and a whistle. If you do get lost you will soon get hungry. The torch may never be needed but will be blessed a thousand times if it is, and if the worst comes to the worst you are more likely to be heard by rescuers than seen. Do make a special point of telling someone where you are going and lastly, but most importantly, use your common sense.

Otmoor (OS 164)

This is a comparatively small area 6 miles north-east of Oxford, bounded by minor roads. The Otmoor towns of Oddington, Charlton, Fencott and Murcott all lie to the north of the moor and all have ready access. Those who wish to approach from the south via Noke or Beckley and hope to ask the way might perhaps care to ponder an ancient Otmoor jingle:

I went to Noke
And nobody spoke.
I went to Beckley
They spoke directly.

Bodmin Moor (OS 200, 201)

The moor is, in effect, split by the A30 which most walkers will wish
to avoid. The northern section contains the higher upland regions of
Rough Tor and Brown Willy, and Camelford is the most convenient
centre for exploration. Cars can be taken from Camelford down
Jubilee Drive to the National Trust car park. There is no equally
obvious starting point for exploration of the southern part of the
moor, but the village of Pensilva (SX/2170) provides a convenient spot
from where the pathway on Caradon Hill can be followed north to
Minions and on to the Cheesewring and Twelve Men's Moor.
Romantics will find Dozmary Pool at SX/195745.

Dartmoor (OS 191, 202)

Dartmoor is ringed by major roads and crossed by the B3212 which,
penetrating as it does the heart of the moor, is a favourite with tourists
– car parking and an information centre can be found at Postbridge
and parking, possibly long term, at Princetown. Those wishing to
explore the southern moor will find car parking at Shipley Bridge (SX/
6863) from where a number of routes may be followed. For the
northern moor, both Sticklepath and Belstone provide attractive
starting points, though there is a lot to be said for approaching the
latter on foot across the moor when it reveals itself as a snug village
folded away into the valley. Haytor rocks are close to a minor road
with parking at SX/7677.

The Ancient Lands (OS 173)

The Marlborough Downs are a comparatively small area well served by
roads. Those who wish to follow a walking route via the Ridgeway
Path can take the minor road south from Wroughton to Barbury Hill
and the earthworks of Barbury Castle (SU/150763). It is assumed that
the reader does not require any assistance in finding Stonehenge.

Mid Wales (OS 136)

The starting point for the author's own walk was the village of
Pennant (SN/880976) but the route followed thereafter and described
in the text cannot be recommended. Instead it is far easier to follow

the river valley to where a zigzag path can be seen climbing the western flank. The path is indicated on the OS map ascending from SN/8795. It leads up to Dylife from where it is a simple matter to follow a route across the plateau and descend by one of the well-marked paths through the woods back down to Pennant.

North Wales (OS 115, OLM Snowdonia)

With such an embarrassment of riches on offer in the Snowdonia region it seems absurd to put forward just the one solitary route. But for those wishing to follow this line the starting point is the Youth Hostel at Ogwen. From here an obvious path leads towards Llyn Idwal and Twll Du where, as described in the text, an ascent of the Glyders can be made. An alternative is to reverse the process and, starting at the same point, head south on the well-marked path past Llyn Bochlwyd for the ridge that leads to the col between Tryfan and Glyder Fach.

Breck, Fen & Marsh (OS 144, 154, 131)

Thetford is the obvious starting point for any exploration of Breckland, and such an exploration should certainly encompass both Thetford Warren and Grimes Graves. The former is criss-crossed by well-defined paths and the latter may be found just off the B1108.

Wicken Fen is a National Trust property located south of the A1123 at Wicken.

The Wash, that great bite out of the east coast of England, is ringed by its sea defences, behind which are the unique marsh lands. It can be approached by any number of routes and the author's own chosen access point of Gedney Drove End is neither better nor worse than many another.

The Peak District (OS 110, 119, OLM The Dark Peak)

The Cromford High Peak Trail is waymarked, and details of the route are available from the Rangers at Middleton Top Engine-House. The rail route proper begins at High Peak Junction (SK/305558). One is tempted to say of the ascent of Kinder Scout: go to Edale and ask anyone in boots to point you towards the Pennine Way. The routes on the hill are well used and well defined, particularly the Pennine Way itself. Details of the route are given in the text.

The Pennines (OS 110, 98, OLM The Three Peaks)

The Colne Valley running west from Huddersfield is so clearly defined as to need little description and there now exists a Colne Valley Walk, taking in the best scenery of the valley and the surrounding moors. It is described in the booklet available in local shops.

Malham offers all facilities for visitors from carpark and information centre to mountain rescue post, the latter a reminder that although this is now a thriving tourist centre, the surrounding hills still hold their dangers. Those wishing to avoid summer crowds might prefer to start at Ingleton, where a path off the B6255 at SD/702731 can be followed up the first of the Three Peaks, Ingleborough.

The Lake District (OS 90, OLM The Lake District)

As with North Wales, there are vast numbers of walks to be selected in the area and anyone intending to spend any length of time in the region should consult one or more of the excellent walking guides. The Langdale Valley itself offers many variations. Routes begin where the road ends at the Old Dungeon Ghyll Hotel. The most popular line follows The Band up the southern side of the valley reached by crossing the Langdale Beck and following the track to Stool End (NY/278057) and on to Bowfell. Alternatively, the northern bank of the beck can be followed to the very steep path up Rossett Gill, which again leads to Bowfell.

The Highlands (OS 56, 50)

A paragraph is insufficient space even to touch on the wealth of Highland countryside, so these notes will be limited to the routes described in the text. Guide books and maps will indicate many hundreds more.

The ascent of the Cobbler begins by the A83 across the loch from Arrochar (NN/288040). The first step of any walks on the upland of Glencoe should be a notification of your route. The actual starting point for the walk undertaken by the author was at NN/182565 beside the A82. The route on Rannoch Moor, has been described in the text, and the moor can be approached either via the turning off the A82 to the King's House Hotel or from the east from Rannoch Station at the end of the B846.

Cape Wrath (OS 9)

The problem of how to approach Cape Wrath is simple, as there is virtually only one way, via the ferry that runs from the Cape Wrath Hotel (NC/378662). Smoo Cave is located at NC/420672. The old peat road to Sandwood Bay is a well-defined track leaving the road at Blairmore (NS/195601). The spectacular scenery around Loch Dionard can be reached by a path that leaves the A838 at NC/310569.

There are many guide books on the market, but the following are all practical guides for walkers which the author has found to be both reliable and useful.

Anderson, J.R.L. and Godwin, Fay: *The Oldest Road: An Exploration of the Ridgeway* 1975
Duerden, Frank: *Great Walks of North Wales* 1982
Galloway, Bruce: *Walks in East Anglia* (2 vols) 1981, 1982
Godwin, Fay and Toulson, Shirley: *The Drovers' Roads of Wales* 1977
Hobson, M.G. and Price K.L.H.: *Otmoor and its Seven Towns* 1961
MacInnes, Hamish: *West Highland Walks* (2 vols) 1979
Pollard, Michael and Ang, Tom: *Walking the Scottish Highlands: General Wade's Military Roads* 1984
Poucher, W.A.: *The Highlands of Scotland* 1983
            The Lake District 1982
            The Peak and Pennines (3rd. ed.) 1978
            The Welsh Peaks (7th ed.) 1979
Rée, Harry and Forbes, Caroline: *The Three Peaks of Yorkshire* 1983
Speakman, Colin: *Walking in the Yorkshire Dales* 1982
Strang, Tom: *The Northern Highlands* (2nd ed.) 1975
Styles, Shinwell: *The Glyder Range* 1974
            The Snowdon Range 1973
Thompson, Clifford: *Walking in the South Pennines* 1979
Toulson, Shirley: *East Anglia: Walking the Ley Lines and Ancient Tracks* 1979
            Derbyshire: Exploring the Ancient Tracks of Mercia 1980
Westacott, Clifford: *Dartmoor for Walkers and Riders* 1983
            The Ridgeway Path 1982
Wright, Christopher John: *A Guide to the Pennine Way* (3rd ed.) 1979

INDEX